POETRY

Kent

Edited by Sarah Washer

First published in Great Britain in 2016 by:

 Young**Writers**

Remus House
Coltsfoot Drive
Peterborough
PE2 9BF
Telephone: 01733 890066
Website: www.youngwriters.co.uk
All Rights Reserved
Book Design by Ashley Janson
© Copyright Contributors 2015
SB ISBN 978-1-78624-006-4

Printed and bound in the UK by BookPrintingUK
Website: www.bookprintinguk.com

Foreword

Welcome, Reader!

For Young Writers' latest competition, *Poetry Emotions*, we gave school children nationwide the task of writing a poem all about emotions, and they rose to the challenge magnificently!

Pupils could either write about emotions they've felt themselves or create a character to represent an emotion. Which one they chose was entirely up them. Our aspiring poets have also developed their creative skills along the way, getting to grips with poetic techniques such as rhyme, simile and alliteration to bring their thoughts to life. The result is this entertaining collection that allows us a fascinating glimpse into the minds of the next generation, giving us an insight into their innermost feelings. It also makes a great keepsake for years to come.

Here at Young Writers our aim is to encourage creativity in children and to inspire a love of the written word, so it's great to get such an amazing response, with some absolutely fantastic poems. This made it a tough challenge to pick the winners, so well done to *Grace Hunt* who has been chosen as the best author in this anthology.

I'd like to congratulate all the young authors in *Poetry Emotions - Kent* - I hope this inspires them to continue with their creative writing.

Jenni Bannister
Editorial Manager

Our charity partner for this academic year is ...

YOUNGMINDS
The voice for young people's **mental health and wellbeing**

We're aiming to raise a huge £5,000 this academic year to help raise awareness for YoungMinds and the great work they do to support children and young people.

If you would like to get involved visit
www.justgiving.com/Young-Writers

YoungMinds is the UK's leading charity committed to improving the emotional wellbeing and mental health of children and young people. They campaign, research and influence policy and practice on behalf of children and young people to improve care and services. They also provide expert knowledge to professionals, parents and young people through the Parents' Helpline, online resources, training and development, outreach work and publications. Their mission is to improve the emotional resilience of all children and to ensure that those who suffer ill mental health get fast and effective support.

www.youngminds.org.uk

Contents

Fleetdown Primary School, Dartford

St Stephen's Primary School, Tonbridge

Scotts Park Primary School, Bromley

Southborough CE Primary School, Tunbridge Wells

Warren Road Primary School, Orpington

The Poems

Phantasmal Fear

Everyone's scared of something,
Now that you have to admit.
Fear is an immortal ghost,
Feasting on our souls.
These invisible devils,
Make audacious heroes weak.
When we are captive to fear,
Tortuous terrors await us.
Fear brings panic to all,
With hair-raising horrors.
So beware, my friends,
Of this spine-chilling fiend.

Haran Subrahmaniyam

I'm A Hungry Man

The hunger of me is very bad
I've been eating five packs of noodles a day
For one day I couldn't eat, hooray!
But then it got worse the following day.

I was so hungry
I was part of the Hungry Heart Club
The following day I left the club
At my house there's a lot of Chinese.

I ate five times a day, three Chineses
Until I ate raw boar and got poisoned
So my mum tried to feed me mustard to make me sick
I didn't want it
So I made a big fuss.

Then I ate some cake, yay!
I was kind of fat,
No, fatter than the world.

Matthew Anderton-Hall (9)
Bishops Down Primary School, Tunbridge Wells

In Memory Of Alfie

Sitting still,
Sad, melancholy memories looming,
Remembering good friends that have left,
Now all I see are sad memories,
I'm swimming in a pool of sadness.

In memory of Alfie.

Everything I see is just a blur,
I see the sun smiling as it goes down,
But when the moon comes up, it's crying
And wanting to see the sun.
The stars tell him not to worry,
He'll be back again tomorrow.

In memory of Alfie.

As I remember everything that has happened,
I remember that everything comes with a
Good memory.
My first time seeing snow,
My first day at school.

In memory of Alfie.

I remember . . .
Opening presents from friends,
Opening presents from Santa,
All my friends at my party,
Having lots of fun.
Then I remember . . .
All the arguments we had,
All the disagreements.
All the great memories,
So as this poem comes to an end.
I know there are still loads more to come.
A single tear rolls down my cheek,
I remember . . .

Alfie.

Molly Purcell
Bishops Down Primary School, Tunbridge Wells

Peak-A-Boo, I Found You

Sneaky, cheeky,
Peek-a-boo, I found you.
Hide-and-seek, all I play,
I go outside every day.
I am a spy to track down someone,
I had a sidekick, but now that's no one.
I go in my car,
Ah, ah,
What has happened?
Peek-a-boo,
I found you.
I get out,
In my mind, doubt.
I heard the chair screaming,
Why was the sun beaming?

I went upstairs
And entered the door of door,
I stopped and looked at the moon.
I opened the door,
Oh no, I'm doomed.
I was too late,
He looked back and said,
'Good luck, old mate.'
I feel like a brick,
Useless,
Why did this happen?
Drums beating in my heart,
But now I feel like this is just the start.

Joshua Vyner (9)
Bishops Down Primary School, Tunbridge Wells

The World Of Anger And Red

Loud noises exploded my head,
Beating drums are screaming instead,
Red as a drip of blood,
So many pounds are hitting my heart,
Hot wax is burning my face,
Fire burning the lava in space.

I had an iron bullet speeding in my brain,
Louder than the longest rain.

Large, ominous ogres have attacked,
My brain is being ransacked.
The red layer is unpeeling,
Divulging scarlet.
Anger has landed,
Steam is a whirlwind,
My life is ending.
The world has entered vermilion red.

A pillar of red light,
Extremely bolt bright,
I am wearing anger glasses,
Ones with lenses of red.

The Devil has entered my heart and my soul,
Burning a wound - a big black hole.

That is my life, full of red flashing lights,
The world of anger and red.

Ava Natalie Robinson (9)
Bishops Down Primary School, Tunbridge Wells

The Ravenous Boy

I walked along a pewter-grey road.
It felt like I haven't had food for years.
My tummy's punching me.
I'm so hungry.
I felt as famished as a T-rex.
I can't take it anymore.
I dropped to the floor.
I found a spider,
I shouldn't have done it,
But I ate it.

I'm hungry, I'm hungry.

As I carried on my walk,
I passed a swimming pool
Of sadness and anger.
But at the end, a swimming pool of food.
I took a big bite,
I was all confused.
I looked around, it was a big, big tree.
This is the end.
I felt my head hit the pristine floor.
I didn't get up.

I'm hungry, I'm hungry.

Oliver Brown (9)
Bishops Down Primary School, Tunbridge Wells

The Tutor

I'm as angry as a raging bull,
Rage is a hurricane,
Entering the doors of anger!
My body is swamped by wind, I'm a hurricane,
The sky will look like a pie
When the demented anger is unleashed!
People like going to the tutor, me, *no!*

I am the angriest you'll ever see me be,
I am an infuriated ball of fire entering the doors of anger.
The remonstrations from the sea of anger enter my brain,
I'm not human anymore, I'm a wolf stampeding towards the horizon.

I wish I was at home you see and I would rather be stung by a bee.
My hands are red, so is my face,
I'm about to scream, 'Get me out of here
Or I'll let my anger unleash!'
I'm a remonstrating, charging lion,
I would watch out if I were you.

Oh no, I'm in trouble,
I'd better run on the double!

Dylan Bridge (9)
Bishops Down Primary School, Tunbridge Wells

The Joy Of Christmas

C hristmas is a good day
H appy and joyful
R acing around the house for so much more
 I hate the part when it all ends
S earching for presents under the tree
T earing apart the wrapping paper is so much fun
M assive amounts of food
A mazing presents
S uch a good day.

Alfie Fraser-W (9)
Bishops Down Primary School, Tunbridge Wells

Sam's Splendid Day

The universe is as wondrous as an awesome place,
I felt as if I had just been to a marvellous place,
My day was obsessed with a football day,
It was full of football in an ecstatic place.

The universe is as wondrous as an awesome place,
I got fish and chips and they were as nice as space.
We thought we were out if we didn't win,
But I scored 2 goals to let us win.
Then we went to Brighton to see some goals,
And we scored two but their goalkeeper played like a moving goal.

The universe is as wondrous as an awesome place,
But my day did finish off with a big blow,
Arsenal lost but at least I felt proud,
I had the best day ever and my life is still young,
But my best day ever is still to come.

I have a lot of events that are still to come,
And I really do still love the world.
To sum it all up of what really happened,
I had my best day ever and it is not the end.

Samuel Gee (9)
Bishops Down Primary School, Tunbridge Wells

Scared In The Darkness

Entering the doors of darkness,
I feel scared.
Illusions of tomorrow,
Dance in my head.
I feel weak,
I don't want a sneak
At what happens tomorrow.

My hazel-brown eyes,
Can't see anything.
The intense sound of silence,
Is very deafening.

The smell of fire,
Burned my entire confidence
Of tomorrow away.

I feel the softest of silks
And taste the creamiest of milks,
But still am not convinced
About tomorrow.

Maya Yildiz (9)
Bishops Down Primary School, Tunbridge Wells

The Joyful Christmas

Christmastime is fun and joyful,
Snow is falling heavily and fast.
Everyone coming together singing songs,
Softly opening presents.
Excitement fills the room.
We all go out heaving snowballs,
Throwing them everywhere.
Snow angels flying afar,
Go back in and play with your new toys,
But it's not the end.

Ella Willmott (9)
Bishops Down Primary School, Tunbridge Wells

Vexation Ruled Over Me!

I entered the dark doors of hell,
Vexation overtook me,
I felt like I had fallen.
I am not confident you see,
So vexation ruled me.

For days, months and years,
Vexation was an emotion that gave me fears.
I tried to slap confidence in me,
But vexation ruled me you see.

As I walked onto the massive stage,
My muscles screamed in protest.
I jumped, I suddenly feel like I had opened
The door of the worry cage.
All my worry flew to the west,
Vexation, it didn't rule me anymore,
I was just like the rest.

Eve Taylor (9)
Bishops Down Primary School, Tunbridge Wells

The Envious And Broken-Hearted Boy

As Olly was leaving the door of death,
He felt disheartened and anxious,
As he opened the great big, mechanical doors of destiny,
He started to flood into treacherous tears,
As he could hear the whistling, waving, thundering wind,
He knew it was the end of the bewildering road.
I could hear the pristine dripping noises running after me,
While they were furiously waving their hands at me
While I was wordlessly waving back.
As we were driving back, I felt melancholy and woebegone,
While I was driving in the dawdling, moulding car.

Oliver Samuel Stewart-Williams (9)
Bishops Down Primary School, Tunbridge Wells

The Happy Holidays

Birthdays are the best, that's right
Best! With your best gifts and your parents' presents
As you tear and glare
As you bounce out of your chair
While holding your teddy bear
Then you sit back down again
And pick up your very own mega bear.

Christmas is great as you go outside and wait
You wait and wait some more
Then some white stuff falls from the sky
And turns everything all white
As you run outside in delight
As you run outside and see everything is all white
Lots of white flakes fall from the sky as you shout joyfully
'Happy holidays!'

Joe Johnson (10)
Bishops Down Primary School, Tunbridge Wells

Silly Is A Calamity

Billy is called Silly,
Silly's brain is as small as a pea.
Silly's brain is also insane.
He opened the door and slammed it shut,
Whilst picking his nose he entered the class of torture.
Silly wanted to go to Mars, but he also liked eating chocolate bars.
Smiley Silly and stupid too,
Then he said, 'I need the loo!'
Don't put mustard on your custard.
He was excitedly jumping, dressed as a kangaroo.
Then he pounced on Anger and screamed, 'Boo!'
Silly's tears were charging down his face
Like rushing reindeers
As his brain was dancing very insanely.

Louis Simmons (9)
Bishops Down Primary School, Tunbridge Wells

Sadness Falls From The Sky

Drip, drip, drip,
Sadness falls from the sky,
Drop, drop, drop,
My tears begin to fly,
Drip, drip, drip,
The rain mixes with my tears,
Drop, drop, drop,
I cry out with fear,
Drip, drip, drip,
The world rushing by like reindeer,
Drop, drop, drop,
My dad's off for about a year,
Drip, drip, drip,
That leaves me alone,
A single tear.

Anna Barker (9)
Bishops Down Primary School, Tunbridge Wells

The Christmas Roast

C alled to my nan's
H urry, it's time to go
R oast is ready
I t's time to eat
S it down, boys, it's time to eat
T ime to go to my dad's
M y dad is home
A pudding is made
S it down, boys, it's pudding time

R eady Dad, can we eat?
O oh, that was yum
A game to play
S orry, Dad, it's time to go
T hat was nice but it's time to go home.

Luca Cureton (9)
Bishops Down Primary School, Tunbridge Wells

Hungry Destruction

Every day of my life I am as hungry as a dinosaur,
Fast food is the best!
I play Hungry Hippo because it makes me feel not so starving.
When I'm hungry it's horrible.
Sometimes I just want to eat everything!
I go outside, smash a building,
Chomp, chomp, chomp, it's all gone.
I've found a candy shop,
Chomp, chomp, chomp, it's all gone.
I went to the cheese shop, I went in.
I couldn't believe my eyes, so much cheese!
I've gone mad with food!
Chomp, chomp, chomp, I ate all of it
But I was still hungry.
What could I eat now?

Hamish Wilson (9)
Bishops Down Primary School, Tunbridge Wells

Getting My Marks Back

The day I got my marks back,
I was as hot as the sun,
My hands were dripping with sweat
And my heart was beating like a drum.

As Mrs Wilson called my name,
I was overcome with fear,
But as she called my name,
The class began to cheer.

I never thought I would score so high,
I was as happy as a clown.
Now I know after a test,
I must never frown.

Codie-Rose Higgins (9)
Bishops Down Primary School, Tunbridge Wells

The Sad Anger

I rage like I'm in a cage,
No one goes near me,
I feel like nobody,
They all make me feel down
But I don't let it show.

They run away when I come,
I feel like a brick,
I'm nothing,
Nobody likes me,
I'm useless.

They all hate me,
Every day my sadness and anger builds up.
So I live underground where there's no sound,
I rage like I'm in a cage.

Ben Clark (9)
Bishops Down Primary School, Tunbridge Wells

The Sea Of Sadness

The world was a sea of worries,
Just sadness, no games,
I felt like I had jumped into a swimming pool of sadness.
My life had no end,
My aquamarine eyes flickered with tears
As blue as a pool on a wet day.
Shouts, screams, more rows and tears,
Suddenly, there is silence.
Nobody wants me,
I feel all alone,
No friend, no home.
I wish I was dead already.

Heather Abrey (9)
Bishops Down Primary School, Tunbridge Wells

An Exciting Day

On my birthday I got lots of presents,
I was so excited, I pranced like a pheasant.
I went to Jamie Oliver's with all of my friends,
They gave us colouring books and a stash of free pens.
Then we had ice cream and sweets galore,
If only Mum had allowed me to give out more.
I felt so excited, I could have cried with laughter,
When I fell over the Pinata.
It was time for my party to come to an end,
I wonder what next year will bring, my friends?

Sophia Smallwood (10)
Bishops Down Primary School, Tunbridge Wells

Guilt Rivers

I know I shouldn't have done it
Those terrible Guilt Rivers flood me
They're already overcoming revenge
Battling the innocence sea

They fill me up with hatred
They've nowhere else to go
As ice, they bite,
As fire, they glow

I see only the raindrops
They are my wretched tears
Of such anger, such guilt!
As this unbearable pain sears

Why, why did I do it?
Every wrongdoing, I mimic
At least I've learnt one thing
Guilt does not unstick.

Emily Astin-Cooke (10)
Bridge & Patrixbourne CE Primary School, Canterbury

Confusion

Confusion is that taste
When Mum overcooks
The roast potatoes.
That taste in your mouth
That stays there forever
Once you've just tried Dad's
Toothpaste.

Confusion looks like a pleading
And longing cat asking for
Spare pork scraps.
A surprised policeman that's been
Accused of a terrible crime.

Confusion feels like sensations
When you have a nightmare
And have found out it was
Just a harmless dream.

Confusion sounds like an . . .
Awkward silence.
It's that time you're trying
To do something well,
Someone whispers,
Then everyone
Starts
Booing!

Jenson North (10)
Bridge & Patrixbourne CE Primary School, Canterbury

Excitement For Christmas

I really, really want a . . .
Bouncy board
But I guess it's too much to afford
Oh well,
Seven more days to go!

I really, really want a . . .
New door
But that's way too much to ask for
Never mind!
Six more days to go!

I really, really want a . . .
Dolly
But it's almost as much as a trolley
Who cares
Five more days to go!

I really, really want a . . .
Sketch book
But only Hank Brook has them
Ohh!
Four more days to go!

I really, really want a . . .
New carpet
But my dog has smelly armpits
It's not the end of the world
Three more days to go!

I really, really want a . . .
Camel
But I think it's a mammal
Oh well!
Two more days to go!

I really, really want a . . .
New top
But there are no good shops
Plop!
One more day to go!

I really, really want . . .
Hold on, it's *Christmas!*
No, it's Father's Day
What?
Christmas is in 312 days
Oh well
312 days to go . . .

Emily Hopkins (10)
Bridge & Patrixbourne CE Primary School, Canterbury

Hope For The Best

Should I do it?
Should I not?
I don't know,
Maybe not.
I'll just give it all I've got.

Let's just hope
For the best,
If I go
Down the slope,
There's always time
To start again.

Nasty nervousness,
Lies on the stage,
I just hope that
I don't fall.
If I do,
Fight back to it,
I don't know,
I'll be fine,
Now it's time.

Christian Muggridge (10)
Bridge & Patrixbourne CE Primary School, Canterbury

Happiness In My Heart

I'm happiness
I am the best
Just nothing more
Or nothing less
As soft as silk
I give out hugs
Now here are some of the things I do
I produce love
I create joy
I fade away the evil feelings
And turn them into truth-telling angels
I fill you up with light and hope
I predict the future
I wash out fear
Filling you up with sunshine and wonder
I'm definitely the best emotion
Nothing could do this, not even a potion.

Felix Archer-Villace (10)
Bridge & Patrixbourne CE Primary School, Canterbury

When I'm Feeling Great!

Do you not have anybody to play with?
What is it?
How old do people live, Mum?
I'm going to do some research about birds outside.
'Can I go on a bike ride tomorrow and take my exploring case?'
Let's have a look around!
Peeking at someone's work at school.
Our pet wolf's attacking the lion again.
I need to investigate!
I am going to explore the Amazon jungle tomorrow!
I'm going to get my magnifying glass out.

A: Curiosity

Rosabelle Bernhardine Amber Smith (7)
Bridge & Patrixbourne CE Primary School, Canterbury

Longing

Longing is the thing that lives in your stomach,
It never lets go,
It makes that feeling always become present,
Fight it away, again and again.
It always comes back,
You can't get rid of it,
You can't hide it behind your back,
It will never go away until you get that hat.

You get that joy,
It goes away,
For a day,
It comes back, pouncing like a cat
Into your stomach.
Here it goes,
The new day,
Slithering slowly past.

Matt McPherson (10)
Bridge & Patrixbourne CE Primary School, Canterbury

The Neglect Corner

Stood there, forgotten
Stood there, alone
Stood there at the door because no one's home.

Sat there, forgotten
Sat there, without concern
Sat there, annoyed because no one's home.

Crouched there, forgotten
Crouched there, left out
Crouched there, in boredom when somebody shouts.

For once, I stand up
For once, I fight back
I feel stronger now, I'm on the right track.

Erin Shenton (10)
Bridge & Patrixbourne CE Primary School, Canterbury

Untitled

I am starting to sweat.
My hands feel like a torrential monsoon,
My hands are the rainclouds, pouring down with sweat.
I'm starting to tremble.
My legs are like a barrel of jelly, wobbling and shaking
Like a tremendous earthquake.
My hands are starting to fidget, I need to stop it now.
So I put my hands in my mouth and start to grind my nails
Like an angry and frustrated beaver.
My arm hairs stick up like towering trees.
My mouth is like the Sahara.
It needs to be cooled down.
I feel like my eyes are about to turn into waterfalls
Dripping like a tap.
What emotion am I?

Nervous.

Miles Packard (8)
Bridge & Patrixbourne CE Primary School, Canterbury

Disgust

The vile scent of smelly socks makes my nose tingle.
When my eyes meet the gross sight of a snotty tissue,
The hairs on my neck stick up on end.
When I glance across the classroom,
One particular person catches my eye.
His finger, planted up his nose, wriggles around for a while
And then stops.
He takes it out and it looms round his lips,
Then quick as a flash, it's gone.
All those things make me shudder and shake,
Put my head in my hands or glance away.
My hair curls and I go pale as a ghost.
My lips dry up and all I can think is *disgust*.

Megan McInnes (10)
Bridge & Patrixbourne CE Primary School, Canterbury

Wondering To The End Of Time

Wonder is an emotion that fills a gap,
Wonder is an emotion that wants a nap,
You may not feel it but it's always there, you start to become unaware,
It makes you dream, it makes you think,
It makes you wonder about an ice hockey rink.
It makes you hunger for sausage and mash,
It makes you hear the waves that crash.

Wonder is like a chicken rap,
To get his attention you need to clap.
Wonder never goes to sleep,
His favourite animal is a sheep.

Wonder is as smart as Einstein himself,
He built a time machine out of a shelf.
Wonder will wonder longer than time,

James McFarlane (10)
Bridge & Patrixbourne CE Primary School, Canterbury

How I'm Feeling

Pet cat attacking our lion, boring.
Sitting in the playground all alone.
When will someone come?
When I have no one to play with
I go to a group of people who are playing a nice game.
Come on someone, come to me!
Will anyone come?
Teacher, you are as bossy as a buffalo, groan, groan.
My feelings are coming back to me!
Teacher blowing the whistle
A whole play-time wasted, oh dear.
'Everyone in, please!'

A: Glum

Annabelle Polly Price Dean (7)
Bridge & Patrixbourne CE Primary School, Canterbury

Morality, Curiosity And Regret

Morality, Curiosity and Regret,
You'd find it difficult I'll bet.
Regret looks behind at our past,
Curiosity gets things done fast.
Morality's our leader, he knows his rights,
We are not seen so much like the nights.
Anger, Happiness and Sadness overlook us,
We're locked on the railway bus.
One day we came out,
With no sign of an angry shout.
We realised they did something wrong,
From then Regret, Curiosity and Morality were pronounced strong.
So now Regret is like a guard,
Curiosity is never hard.
Morality teaches good and bad,
And now no emotion will be sad.

Mackenzie Lynch (9)
Bridge & Patrixbourne CE Primary School, Canterbury

How Am I Feeling?

I look left, I look right
I am the opposite to bright
I am as lost as a fly
I am the emotion that can't walk to you that easily
My mind gets fuzzy and I feel like I'm in a maze
Meaning I can't find what to say
I hardly ever find my way
I turn pale, I turn white
I look up at the grown-ups
I look down at the floor
I feel like a piece of a puzzle that can't find where to go.
What emotion am I?

Puzzled

Rosie Newton (8)
Bridge & Patrixbourne CE Primary School, Canterbury

Rage

Rage lives deep down inside.
He is the thing stopping your smile.
The thing barricading your laughter.
The thing caging your confidence
And flooding the roads with fear.

His head is on fire with nightmares.
His terrifying torso is torn.
His arms and legs are boiling
And his back is a swarm of thorns.

He only comes out when joy is in doubt
So not to be spotted by other emotions.
The only way to beat him is take deep breaths in.
For rage doesn't breathe air.
And when he tastes it in the back of his throat,
He'll go away for days!

Charlie Kirk (9)
Bridge & Patrixbourne CE Primary School, Canterbury

Stress Is . . .

Stress is creepy and crammed,
It's also the thing I hate most,
Stress is a life full of mayhem,
Amethyst is the colour of anxiety.

Stress is rushed and annoying,
But stress is also the feeling,
When you haven't done your
Homework.

Stress is terrifying to think about,
Stress is annoying and painful,
But worst of all,
Stress strikes
Argh!

Oscar Cameron (9)
Bridge & Patrixbourne CE Primary School, Canterbury

Is Arrogance So Bad?

If I am the burden of arrogance
Am I so bad?
So what if I have a
Superior intellect?
So what if I'm super speedy?
So what if all their timid, feeble minds
Can't comprehend my cleverness?
Is it my fault I'm so outstandingly brilliant?
So what if my memorable arrogance is as astonishing
As my titanium cranium made from potassium?

So here you go world, here's some sense!
Bang! Clang! Clonk! Crack!
That's what you deserve
Hmmm . . .
Am I so bad?

Joshua Lee O'Sullivan (10)
Bridge & Patrixbourne CE Primary School, Canterbury

Anger

I think my ears are going to blow up,
Fire alarm going off,
So annoying.
I don't think my rage
Can hide from the
Seeker.
I'm sweating, I'm going as red as an
Apple.
Then I blurt something out,
That I did not
Want to say.
Now I wish I did not
Let my anger spill
Out!

Tom McAllister (10)
Bridge & Patrixbourne CE Primary School, Canterbury

Guilt

Stolen what is not yours
To sit in the corner with chattering jaws
Of your house of stolen bricks
Pushing you away from the wall with gentle kicks

Stolen what is not yours
Locking up all your doors
Forget about your sins
And throw them in the bins

Stolen what is not yours
You must abide with the laws
The floor gives you a poke
The rotten egg on the floor
The yolk being the boat

You finally write a little sorry note.

Sam Taylor Easterbrook (10)
Bridge & Patrixbourne CE Primary School, Canterbury

Fear

Being afraid makes me melt,
It is one of the things I have always felt,
When I feel fear,
I put up with it,
But when it hurts,
I can't help but feel fear forever with it.

When I am afraid,
I don't hide it,
But when I get home,
I will tell about it.
When I get afraid,
I don't lie,
When I get happy,
I never sigh.

Harrison Baillie White (10)
Bridge & Patrixbourne CE Primary School, Canterbury

Fear

I am cold sweat, I am your nightmare,
What am I?
I am butterflies in your stomach, I am churning in your tummy,
What am I?
I am hiding in a cave getting ready to pounce,
I am always there no matter where you turn,
What am I?
I am wandering round the corner when you least expect it,
I am soaring through your head,
What am I?
I am goosebumps, I am your hair standing on end,
What am I?
I am shivers up your spine,
I am flying through the whistling wind to catch you off guard,
What am I?

Tom Hutton (10)
Bridge & Patrixbourne CE Primary School, Canterbury

The Nightmare

The room is dark
There is no light
The darkness goes round
I close my eyes with all my might.

Darkness comes watching me
It comes towards me, staring
Shadows jump and bite and scratch like wild animals
I fall down a hole of darkness.

I wake up, the light reassures me
The trees stretch in the morning wind
Happiness is precious I think
I hope the nightmare never comes again.

William Richards (10)
Bridge & Patrixbourne CE Primary School, Canterbury

I Am Anger

I am anger.
I get the hump.
Say if someone gave me a bump.
I am anger.
I am red.
Especially when Mum tells me to go to bed.
I am anger.
I am fire.
I am you when you've got a flat tyre.
I am anger.
I am furious.
I am something you don't find luxurious.
I am anger
I am an angry grin.
I am you when your son throws your phone in the bin.

Tom Shaw (9)
Bridge & Patrixbourne CE Primary School, Canterbury

Anger Is . . .

My emotions are like a flaming, fat, big fire,
Also the frustration flowing in a pile,
The coal's ready to be chucked in a fire,
To make it big and higher.

The emotion anger won't stay in forever,
In the red, bold, flaming castle,
The nightmares awaken, screaming out loud,
Like a bomb about to explode, big like a bang.

It feels like bubbling, boiling water,
Burning and erupting in the big volcano,
Anger is the nightmares, screaming out loud,
It is the wolves howling and keeping the children up.

Leah Roshel Scantlebury (9)
Bridge & Patrixbourne CE Primary School, Canterbury

Joy

Whenever I am joyful,
I'll jump up and down,
I'll take away your sorrow,
I'll take away your frown.

Whenever I am joyful,
You'll see it on my lips,
I'll smile ear to ear,
It's a smile you won't miss.

Whenever I am joyful,
I'll be helpful as can be,
I'll spread my smile to you,
You'll be happy, with me.

Alicia Nielsen Gorgojo (10)
Bridge & Patrixbourne CE Primary School, Canterbury

Guilt Is Grey

Guilt is grey and will always stay,
Something you can never get rid of,
It won't go away and will always say,
'Hey, you didn't do something you should have!'

It's like a dark shadow lurking at
The back of your head and has hollow lines
Underneath its eyes from tossing
And turning in bed.

It's a stormy sea churning up your stomach,
Something you wouldn't go near,
Something you know sooner or later,
Will become a drastic fear.

Hephzibah Harvey (10)
Bridge & Patrixbourne CE Primary School, Canterbury

Nervousness

Nervousness came up from inside
From the dark caves of sadness
Tiptoeing out to creep you
Stunning you with its meaningful stare

The worst of them when you're about to do something
Is always there but is not out
Nervousness jumps out and traps you with it
Its dark purple lair is where you will stay

For hours on end you're trapped in the dark
Because
Nervousness is out
Beware, don't shout!

Poppy Bostock (9)
Bridge & Patrixbourne CE Primary School, Canterbury

My Emotion Poem

My face and hands go red-hot.
I get wound up.
My teeth are crunching together.
Every time my face squints.
I get really hot.
Steam comes out of my ears.
It makes me want to lose energy.
Sometimes it makes me cry.
It makes me feel like my tummy's a tumble dryer
Going round and round.

What emotion am I?
I am anger.

Cian Lidbury (7)
Bridge & Patrixbourne CE Primary School, Canterbury

Anger Actions

I clench my teeth as hard as I can.
My face rages bright red.
I feel like I want to slam a door as hard as I can.
My face feels like a scrunched up piece of paper in a bin.
I am red hot.
I am getting sweaty and my clothes stick to me
And I am getting annoyed.
I screw my fists up like I'm going to punch someone.
I am the 'get out of the way' emotion.
I am the emotion you do not want to meet.
What emotion am I?

A: Anger.

Charlie Roberts (8)
Bridge & Patrixbourne CE Primary School, Canterbury

What Emotion Am I?

I feel like a red-hot chilli pepper
Coming out of a volcano

You would not like to be my personality
Because I will make you . . .
Shout!

I am the lump of molten lava that will creep up your throat
And make you react in a fuming way.

You will not like your reaction.

What emotion am I?

A: Fury.

Angus Goddard (8)
Bridge & Patrixbourne CE Primary School, Canterbury

Anxiety

N erves, cautiously cuddling to the sound of the applause
E very pair of eyes, focused on me
R apidly, my helpless heart pounds to the beat of a drum
V ery bright ruby-red face blushing a scarlet-red
E yes watering
R ehearsing my routine in nerves
A nxiety building up inside of me
C urdling blood huddling from the shaking hand
K eeping courage before it fades away
 I n fear as the cameras shoot out
N ot focused on the routine anymore!
G oing on stage . . . wish me luck!

Katie Vince (10)
Bridge & Patrixbourne CE Primary School, Canterbury

Anger

I am angry at that blast that hit Earth and doomed dinos.
I wanted a pet one.
I am angry at those sailors who ate the dodo.
I wanted to eat them.
I am angry at the cavemen because they ate mammoths.
They went extinct.
Anger of anger.
Mean of mean.
Terror of terror.
I am angry at the war.
I wanted to beat them.
End anger.

Robert Parry (9)
Bridge & Patrixbourne CE Primary School, Canterbury

I Am Always Fearless

I could defend like a guard dog
Ready to protect my owner.

I stand very strong
And I am never to be afraid.

I can touch a dangerous animal.
I have tons of courage.

My hands can be tough and strong
I am like a lightning bolt striking down below.

I am so intrepid
I can walk into the creepiest wood.

Anna Hanzlik (9)
Bridge & Patrixbourne CE Primary School, Canterbury

Sadness

Sadness is a fire that doesn't spread,
Sadness is an emotion that people dread.

Sadness means someone's hurt or scared,
Sadness is something which people dared.

Sadness comes and goes,
Sadness creates your woes.

Sadness is something that hides away,
Sadness will always stay.

Sadness is something that makes you cry,
But with one big breath you can try.

Thomas Roberts (10)
Bridge & Patrixbourne CE Primary School, Canterbury

Untitled

I am the hot and flushed face
I'm as pink as a dress
My brain is screaming, *run away*
But I just stand there still
It's the time of day when I'm not proud
I sweat and stare at other people
I am the, 'Oh no' and 'I'm so sorry.'
I am the big gasp that everyone hears
I am the rosy red cheeks.

What emotion am I?
Embarrassed.

Ava Goddard (8)
Bridge & Patrixbourne CE Primary School, Canterbury

My Emotion Poem

I feel strong.
I'm as tall as a tree.
My face is burning hot.
My legs are as good as new.
I know what I'm doing.
I'm never frightened because I'm brave!
I try new things.
I don't get worried.
I will be strong forever.
I will never die.

I'm brave.

Hollie-Marie Finch (8)
Bridge & Patrixbourne CE Primary School, Canterbury

What Am I?

I am as jumpy as a young rabbit in the spring.
I am the sort of person you want to meet.
I am on holiday being happy.
I am starting to go crazy and out of control.
My body is stretching like a stretchy figure
Because I keep reaching for the sky.
I have aching legs because I keep jumping for joy.
I am so happy because I am kind,
Do good work and get lots of marbles.
What emotion am I?

A: Excited

Isabella Hubbard (8)
Bridge & Patrixbourne CE Primary School, Canterbury

My Emotions

I am the smile on the face and the narrowing of the eyes.
I am the happy and joyful person who can't stop talking rapidly.
I can't stop jumping around and the time is going too slowly
Because I am waiting.
I get bursts of bubbles from head to toe.
I am like a dog wagging its tail for a bone.
I get a tingly feeling inside my body.
My arms are doing jazz hands and I don't know why.
But I feel like I will touch the sky.
What emotion am I?

Excited.

Ruby Keem (8)
Bridge & Patrixbourne CE Primary School, Canterbury

How I'm Feeling!

Ahhhhhhhh!
Leaping lizards
Run for your life
My face is as red as a shiny apple
No way!
Watch out
Where am I?
What's going on?
What emotion is it?
My head is playing tricks on me.

Paranoid

Beth McInnes (7)
Bridge & Patrixbourne CE Primary School, Canterbury

A Grin Came To My Cheeky Face

My feet were jogging on the spot, ready to run for it.
I am a bull charging at a red cloth.
A voice in my head tells me to go for it.

I haven't got a care in the world.
I am the 'I'm just gonna go for it' in your life.
Everything begs me to use it.
It is obvious what I'm about to do before I do it.

I am what you are when you are excited.
What emotion am I?

A: Carefree

Yasir Alhassan (8)
Bridge & Patrixbourne CE Primary School, Canterbury

Nervousness

N asty thoughts running through my head
E specially worried and quiet
R ed as a tomato
V ery concerned
O nly looking on the bad side of it
U pset, uncertain
S ticky, sweating hands
N ot cheerful, chirpy
E xtra hot
S uper butterflies build up inside
S haking as much as a snake.

Esme Brown (10)
Bridge & Patrixbourne CE Primary School, Canterbury

Curiosity

If you want to find something out,
I will help you without a doubt.
I make you confused,
As you try to find out clues.
If you don't know what something is,
I help you find out in a whizz.
You could be stuck in a mess
And you might just have to guess
What is lurking behind the wall,
Maybe it is something scary and tall.
What am I?

William Artingstoll-Meloy (9)
Bridge & Patrixbourne CE Primary School, Canterbury

That's What Guilt Thinks

Should I have done that?
Was that the right thing to do?
That's what Guilt thinks
What shall I do?
Tell a teacher?
Go apologise
Or leave it?
That's what Guilt thinks
Why did I do that?
Should I own up?
That's what Guilt thinks.

Elliott King (10)
Bridge & Patrixbourne CE Primary School, Canterbury

Fury Is A Path

Fury is a path to many different things.
If it takes control of you, you'll have lots of mood swings.
It starts off small, sly and weak,
But if it gets to your brain,
It will really make you squeak.
And if he's still not gone, I'll give you this advice,
Try to picture him as something nice.
Fury is a path to the dark side,
Fury is the path to hate,
Fury is a route to suffering,
And worst of all, fury is a path to eternal sorrow.

Silas Jacob Franks (10)
Bridge & Patrixbourne CE Primary School, Canterbury

How I'm Brave

I am as brave as a bullet shooting through the air.
I'm fighting fierce villains as I go.
When there's someone in trouble,
My hands tingle like the sound of a rattlesnake
And I run to the rescue.
Saving princesses, princes and people is my job.
I never sleep at midnight.
My face tells me I can't because someone is in trouble.
I save everyone, even the Queen in her royal palace.

Courageous.

Jessica Cowley (7)
Bridge & Patrixbourne CE Primary School, Canterbury

My Emotion Poem

I am shaking and I am alone.
I am paranoid and jumpy like a kangaroo.
I am surprised and puzzled.
I am dead still like a statue.
I am shocked and confused.
When I'm shaky, I sweat.
I am disorganised.
My tummy does cartwheels.
My mind plays up.

A: Petrified

Anya Louise Mackenzie (7)
Bridge & Patrixbourne CE Primary School, Canterbury

Untitled

I could probably cheer you up if you are sad.
I am in the mood that I don't go mad.
I am the person you would want to meet.
I am the type of person you would go out with to eat.
I have this really good feeling in my mouth,
That we should be heading south.
I am the opposite of grumpy.
I have a lovely big smile.
What emotion am I?

I am excitement!

Katie Back (8)
Bridge & Patrixbourne CE Primary School, Canterbury

Pride

When I'm proud, I'll be a balloon of joy,
When my work is on the wall, I am honoured,
When I finish long hours of homework, satisfaction is here,
I feel happy and excited when I am proud,
When you are proud, you should be pleased.

Pride is a crown, sitting on my head,
Pride is my face on a TV screen,
Pride is the trophy glistening in the light,
Pride is normally a positive feeling but if you start to boast,
You would find yourself alone . . .

Finn Sennett (9)
Bridge & Patrixbourne CE Primary School, Canterbury

YoungWriters

Untitled

I am a dictionary, repeating the same words over and over again.
I am tiptoeing into an old, abandoned house just to see what is inside.
I am as excited as a chimpanzee with mangoes.
I get fiddly.
My eyes expand.
My face expands, my fingers twitch and my eyes tingle.
I want to explore.

What emotion am I?
Curious.

Sophie Fulljames (9)
Bridge & Patrixbourne CE Primary School, Canterbury

What Am I?

You think of me when you think of space,
I make you feel so different,
So lost and unusual on the big roller coaster of life,
My mouth might go as dry as a bone,
And I might shout, 'No!' when friends ask for a loan,
I'm not happy-go-lucky, not at all,
To amuse myself I might try throwing a ball,
You think of me all lost and alone,
But just remember, you're never alone.

What am I?

Becky Cook (8)
Bridge & Patrixbourne CE Primary School, Canterbury

Who Am I?

Am I fear do you think?
But I don't panic with fire-red.
So am I depression and runaway with sea-blue tears on my face?
But I am not these things so I'll be proud with perfect purple.
But in the end I will be one.
One of those people who bully.
So now there's only one choice.
I am joy, I am excitement with delight.
I am always positive so this is what I want to be.
Happy!

Charlotte Richards (9)
Bridge & Patrixbourne CE Primary School, Canterbury

Opposites Are Equal

I am your favourite animal,
Running on rigid terrain,
Swimming in the vast azure blue,
Flying through the air, wings in the clouds.
I am the sparkling waters of a waterfall,
Falling graciously into the clear, sapphire, placid lake.
I am ying and yang dressed in deep cobalt and emerald-green.
I am the Titanic, sailing joyfully,
With the wind howling from port to starboard.
I am one step for man, one giant leap for mankind.

Daniel Stevens (10)
Bridge & Patrixbourne CE Primary School, Canterbury

Nervousness

'Going on stage in 3, 2, 1.'
I can see the audience, their eyes glued tightly to the stage,
My glittering bun in my shimmering hair and gleaming make-up
Makes me look graceful.
What about my costume? Purple and orange,
It might be too short or too long.
Now it's showtime, oh my gosh,
I've forgotten my words, I've forgotten my words.
What am I going to do?
Then the audience *clap, clap, clap.*

Issi Linnane (9)
Bridge & Patrixbourne CE Primary School, Canterbury

Horror

Horror gives me fear that I just hate to hear.
It pops out at night, I just hate its sight.
It slumps and it creeps, it walks and it peeps.
It howls at night and it hides at light.
It sleeps in the day and goes its own way.
It whispers in your ear, saying, 'Fear.'
It walks around, underground.
It waits like an ounce, ready to pounce.
Until the moon comes soon.
Beware my friend, it's going to pounce like an ounce!

Jadon Pereira (9)
Bridge & Patrixbourne CE Primary School, Canterbury

My Poem

I glow like the sunny hot days in the summer time.
I am happy all the time.
I am the best smiley girl ever.
I will put a smile on your lovely face.
I like wearing a bow.
I like being happy all the time.
I am the emotion that you like to meet.

What emotion am I?
Joyful.

Daisie Fisher (8)
Bridge & Patrixbourne CE Primary School, Canterbury

Untitled

I can feel my body getting hotter on the inside,
I turn redder and redder and redder.
I am a hot, spicy chilli.
I am like a bull when you hold up a red card.
Eventually I get as hot as a bubbling volcano.
I start to turn purple.
You would never like to see or speak to me.
What emotion am I?

Fury.

Anna Muggridge (8)
Bridge & Patrixbourne CE Primary School, Canterbury

My Emotion

I feel like this at my house and my nanny's house at weekends.
My hands tingle.
I also feel like this at Easter, Christmas and my birthday.
I almost burst.
I am as jumpy as a kangaroo.
My face lights up and I get a butterfly in my tummy.
School trips make me feel like this.
What emotion am I?

Excited.

Gracie Loren Trott (7)
Bridge & Patrixbourne CE Primary School, Canterbury

Worry

F ear follows
I nteresting ideas
R aiding ring
E mergency exit

A nxiety awakes
L ots of concern
A nxiety awakes
R umours raid
M oving memories.

Max Wright (10)
Bridge & Patrixbourne CE Primary School, Canterbury

My Emotion

I heard the music playing as loud as a lion.
I felt like I was dreaming!
My eyes grow wider and wider, I almost burst.
My body glowed like sunshine on the hottest day of the year!
I jumped in the air like a kangaroo.
I had butterflies, but in a good way.
I love days like this.

What emotion am I?
Excited.

Arabella Stanley (7)
Bridge & Patrixbourne CE Primary School, Canterbury

Untitled

I am like a sleeping bear.
I am as grumpy as a grizzly bear.
I feel like a waste of time.
I am as silent as a koala.
I appear at the weekends
When I have absolutely nothing to do.
I slouch and moan, 'errrrr.'
What emotion am I?

A: Bored

Joel Murray (8)
Bridge & Patrixbourne CE Primary School, Canterbury

I Am Hope

I am the one that helps you believe.
I am the one that gives you happiness.
I cross my fingers like 'cross keys.'
I smile a kind smile.
I am as strong as a tiger.
No one can destroy me, no one.
I am the one that makes you strong.
Without me you'll be nothing.

Who am I?

Rebecca Lawal (8)
Bridge & Patrixbourne CE Primary School, Canterbury

Feelings

My belly is a bundle of butterflies.
I come out when something unusually bad happens.
My body vibrates with fear.
A lump suddenly starts growing like a hill in my throat.
There's a knot as big as a boulder in my stomach.
My brain won't let me stop thinking about the terrible thing that
happened.
What emotion am I?

Worried.

Chester Renham (8)
Bridge & Patrixbourne CE Primary School, Canterbury

Untitled

My eyes are damp and red
My heart is broken in two
I am crying, tears run down my cheek
Like raindrops on a window
My head is buried in the table
There is a dark cloud that cloaks me
Like a blanket.
What emotion am I?

Sad!

Holly Brown (8)
Bridge & Patrixbourne CE Primary School, Canterbury

Hope

Hope is the despairing sea,
Beaten by the rain.

But Hope saves the day,
Repelling the rain again.

Hope is the rising sun,
Covered by the clouds.

But Hope again is present,
Sending the clouds crying aloud.

Deji Lawal (10)
Bridge & Patrixbourne CE Primary School, Canterbury

Regret

Regret lives in a mysterious place
Whispering at you to run and hide
Honour and dishonour tug at you
Regret is a grey-blue scroll
Torn up and tattered
Regret is a tiny grey monster
Miserable and hurt
His small voice squeaks
'Why did you do it?'

Benjamin Paxton (9)
Bridge & Patrixbourne CE Primary School, Canterbury

Joy

Joy is buttercups in the meadow,
Joy lets my spirit run free,
I need to catch my spirit now,
I am at the top of a green hill staring blankly at the blue sky,
Joy reminds me of my happy friends,
Joy reminds me of pleased God and caring Jesus, smiling down at me,
Joy is a flock of white doves flying towards the sun,
I love joy, I will never forget it.

Ashlyn Stodart (9)
Bridge & Patrixbourne CE Primary School, Canterbury

Anxiety

Anxiety is that blood-curdling voice
Running through your stomach yelping . . .
'Get me out of here!'
Anxiety is the nerve that boils and pops
Causing butterflies to swarm.
Anxiety is your heart bubbling up in excitement.
Anxiety is gnashed nails scattered on the floor.
Anxiety is your mum when she screams at you and cries,
'Eat those sprouts!'

Matthew Oji (9)
Bridge & Patrixbourne CE Primary School, Canterbury

My Emotions Poem

Feeling frightened,
I really don't want to do that.
I am wobbly like jelly.
Growing more and more afraid.
Hungry feelings and terrified.
Everyone is OK except me.
Eating is impossible.
Danger ahead.
What emotion am I?

JJ Bury (7)
Bridge & Patrixbourne CE Primary School, Canterbury

What Am I?

I cross my arms.
I am rolling my eyes like a runaway marble.
My legs flop like a dog's tongue.
I'm a 'don't care' and a 'whatever' person.
I barely battle the needs of others.
I'm a nasty old humbug and disgrace to this world.

What emotion am I?

Careless.

Dylan Pollard (8)
Bridge & Patrixbourne CE Primary School, Canterbury

My Feelings

My face feels like a slow snowball.
I feel like a roller coaster going round and round.
My hands are so hot it feels like they're a desert.
I feel like a small mouse.
I feel like I will throw up.
My body is very shaky.

What am I?
I am nervous.

Louis Cussen (7)
Bridge & Patrixbourne CE Primary School, Canterbury

What Emotion Am I?

My smile is as big as an oversized banana!
I didn't know I could do this before.
My parents are amazed, they couldn't do this like I'd done it.
I can feel happiness bubbling up my throat.
I am a lion, my glorious mane is swishing in the wind.
I feel like I could burst with joy!

What emotion am I?
Proud.

Madeleine Spencer (8)
Bridge & Patrixbourne CE Primary School, Canterbury

My Emotion Poem

When a nightmare keeps me awake, I hold my teddies tightly.
A river of my tears as I climb up high.
Shouting as loud as a lion's roar makes me tremble.
When someone jumps out at me, I fall to the wall.
My hands and face go pale.
When I fall off a high slide, I close my eyes.
What emotion am I?

A: Terrified

Ethan Thomas McFarlane (7)
Bridge & Patrixbourne CE Primary School, Canterbury

My Emotion Poem

My head is so crazy, smoke is coming out of my head.
There's thunder coming through the clouds.
I am angry!
My door is getting crunched up, it's pouring down.
My teeth are getting much bigger.
I am angry!
What emotion am I?

A: Anger

James Nicholas Spicer-Hale (7)
Bridge & Patrixbourne CE Primary School, Canterbury

Untitled

I am your sun, your moon,
Your words, your tune, your Earth,
Your sky, your sea,
I am everything to you,
I am your bright light in the darkness,
I am your peace and happiness,
I am also your special person.

What am I?

Loreta Tunbridge (8)
Bridge & Patrixbourne CE Primary School, Canterbury

What Am I?

You bring me to a party,
You see me when you are jolly,
You use me to giggle like a hyena,
I love being happy,
People love my emotion,
I put a bright smile on your face,
And turn that frown upside down.

What am I?

Isabella Hancock (8)
Bridge & Patrixbourne CE Primary School, Canterbury

My Day

I feel like I am going to burst,
Today is my day.
It's the day I've always wanted.
My hands are on my cheeks,
My hair is waving all over the place.
This day will never end.
Who am I?

Excited

Roxanne McCormack (9)
Bridge & Patrixbourne CE Primary School, Canterbury

Untitled

You often look in the sky when you feel me,
With a big smile on your face,
My name is mentioned at Christmas time,
And I am close to happy,
You would feel me in summer as well,
When you're out in the sunshine,
I make you jump up in the air.

What am I?

Camille Hoberg (8)
Bridge & Patrixbourne CE Primary School, Canterbury

My Emotion Poem

I am so jumpy, like a kangaroo
My eyes are growing wider and wider and they are nearly popping
out
I am not tired at all
Jumping like a frog in my tummy
This is going to be so much fun
I love this time!

Excited

Amelie Bostock (7)
Bridge & Patrixbourne CE Primary School, Canterbury

Untitled

When the teacher is teaching something new
That I don't understand
My hands are tall tree branches
My nose all crinkled up
My head goes blank
My vision fuzzy
The worry of it reminds me of smoke.

What am I?

Kate Milly Mannings (9)
Bridge & Patrixbourne CE Primary School, Canterbury

What Am I?

I was banging the table and stomping my feet
I could not stop punching the air
I could feel sweat trickling down my neck
I was boiling hot
I started to feel very tough
My face went bright red
My head was aching because I was annoyed
I threw my Xbox on the floor!

Rafael Archer-Villace (8)
Bridge & Patrixbourne CE Primary School, Canterbury

Sadness

I am sad when it rains on a dark cloudy day,
When it rains like cats and dogs.
I don't like school because I am always sad,
And I am bullied and I can't even add 1+1, it's so hard.
I think sadness is a deep, dark sea of loneliness,
With no life but with just sad lives.
I hate Christmas, all of the bother of the dinner.
That's what sadness is.

Charlotte Streeting (9)
Bridge & Patrixbourne CE Primary School, Canterbury

Disgust

Disgust is the green face of sickness,
Disgust is stomach acid burning in my throat,
Disgust is the slimy mess on the floor,
Disgust is a scrunched up face.
Disgust is a squashed body on the roadside,
Disgust is a mush of out-of-date food,
Disgust is someone eating cottage cheese,
Disgust is homeless people's food.

Kaleb Josiah Denison (10)
Bridge & Patrixbourne CE Primary School, Canterbury

My Emotion Poem

I am frightened when I go past a graveyard at night on my own,
Tears drip down my red, frightened face.
I go really numb like an ice block.
I scream for my mum and dad.
They wake up and snuggle me up and I calm down a bit.
I begin with P and end with D.
What emotion am I?

Beatrix Bainbridge (7)
Bridge & Patrixbourne CE Primary School, Canterbury

My Feelings

Sometimes when it's sports day I get terrified!
I feel a bit jumpy
A bit like I'm going to cry.
I'm as shy as a mouse.
Sometimes I need a friend to cheer me up.
My hands feel all wet
I begin with N and end with S.
What am I?

Ilana Grace Lord (8)
Bridge & Patrixbourne CE Primary School, Canterbury

My Super Emotion Poem!

My body feels empty like a car that's run out of petrol.
I feel like this when I've walked for hours.
I want to sleep peacefully for the rest of the day.
No energy like a broken bulb.
When I've finished my work, busy as a bee,
I feel like this.
Everything seems harder!
What emotion am I?

Kaya Clark (7)
Bridge & Patrixbourne CE Primary School, Canterbury

Nervousness Is . . . ?

Nervousness is walking onto a burning hot stage while everybody turns silent.
Nervousness is your body telling you run, run.
Nervousness is your body shaking itself.
Nervousness is the most unpredictable thing.
Nervousness is your first day at a new school.
Nervousness is taking a penalty to win the whole game.

Joseph Alexander Palmer (9)
Bridge & Patrixbourne CE Primary School, Canterbury

I Feel Anger

Anger is a potion bubbling up inside you.
Anger is sad and never happy.
Anger is a loud, fiery bang
That you scream at someone to make them sad.
Anger is a blazing forest fire that never dies
And destroys everything ahead.
Anger will be an explosion
When the bomb goes off!

Sacha Buss (9)
Bridge & Patrixbourne CE Primary School, Canterbury

Thrilled

Today I get thrilled by a new theme park ride.
Today I get thrilled by a brand new movie.
Today I get thrilled by a new species.
Today I get thrilled by my learning a new kung-fu move.
Today I get thrilled by a race and I win.
Today I get thrilled by an orchestra playing the violin.
Today I get thrilled by everything.
What do you get thrilled by?

Oscar Griffiths (9)
Bridge & Patrixbourne CE Primary School, Canterbury

Nervous

N o idea what to do.
E veryone knows what is happening but me.
R eally scared.
V ery big avalanche rolling down the mountain.
O h, no! What is going to happen?
U nhappy like a lonely mole.
S tarting something new.

Ben Griffiths (7)
Bridge & Patrixbourne CE Primary School, Canterbury

Anger

Anger is the burst of adrenaline that accelerates your fist.
Anger is the pure black ink on a perfect page.
Anger is the rancid bully blaming you for something you didn't do.
Anger is a burning inferno inside, struggling to get out.
Anger is a question you can't answer.
Anger is a cupcake you're not allowed to eat.
Anger is a mirror with a fire reflection.
Anger is a golden bullet zooming through the smoky air.

Alfie Ennis (9)
Bridge & Patrixbourne CE Primary School, Canterbury

Untitled

I turn my back and walk far away,
I want some time on my own,
I really want to cry and wail,
I'm as hurt as a lame horse.
Others' words turn me to tears as I fall to the ground,
My mouth grows wide, as my tongue transforms to dry.
I think they say those words to make me feel this emotion.
What am I?

Michael Nkereuwem (8)
Bridge & Patrixbourne CE Primary School, Canterbury

What Makes A Happy Friend?

What makes a happy friend?
Is it someone who's joyous?
What makes a happy friend?
Is it someone who's mad?
What makes a happy friend?
Will it be someone who's happy or joyous?
Will it be someone who's good or bad?

Archie Hatcher (10)
Bridge & Patrixbourne CE Primary School, Canterbury

Loss

Loss is a piercing feeling living inside you,
Loss strongly destroys all positive emotions,
Loss is a stick pounding your back, making you fall,
Loss is your heart pounding and you lose all your hope,
Loss is your mind barking with sadness,
Loss is an everlasting removal,
Loss is a strong parting in you,
Loss is letting a deep cry of burning fire blazing inside.

Jens Chappell (9)
Bridge & Patrixbourne CE Primary School, Canterbury

Brave

I stand confident and strong.
Nothing worries me.
I am like a strong tsunami raging through the sky.
I am determined to achieve.
I'm as strong as a rhino.
I stand as bold as a knight.

What emotion am I?

Benjamin Farnham (8)
Bridge & Patrixbourne CE Primary School, Canterbury

Emotions

I never ever cry, even when I feel like it.
You might feel me when you go on holiday.
You feel me when you're at a funfair.
You feel me when you see someone you really like.
I am a happy feeling to be.
I am like happy.
Who am I?

Oscar Sands (7)
Bridge & Patrixbourne CE Primary School, Canterbury

What Emotion Am I?

I feel excited
I hold my head up high
I stand tall
I have relaxed shoulders
I want to be seen
I know I can do it!

What emotion am I?

Toby Plumb (8)
Bridge & Patrixbourne CE Primary School, Canterbury

Untitled

You can see me when people annoy me.
I have fire on my head and steam coming out my ears.
I always grit my teeth.
My mind is exploding like a bomb.
I appear when people are mean to me and I stomp off.

What emotion am I?
Anger.

Connor Cooke (8)
Bridge & Patrixbourne CE Primary School, Canterbury

Helpful, Helpful

H elp people who need it most
E xciting times are like love forever
L ove can never end
P eaceful people make life a calmer place
F ull of happiness to make others laugh
U sually you give people a smile and that makes them happy
L augh and they will laugh back.

Poppy Hubbard (10)
Bridge & Patrixbourne CE Primary School, Canterbury

What Am I?

I might make you hurt someone.
I might make you get warmer and warmer like an oven.
I might make you chuck something.
I sometimes make you break stuff like a T-rex eating a human.
I make you out of control.
You can give this emotion to someone else but it's not worth it.

What am I?

Hussayn Shirazi (8)
Bridge & Patrixbourne CE Primary School, Canterbury

Anger

Anger is a cloud full of roaring thunder.
Anger is a bomb that explodes to a single touch.
Anger is when your mum says no!
Anger is flowing hot lava bursting out a volcano.

Anger is the sound of orange clashing tigers.
Anger is the burnt black potatoes.
Anger is when you don't get your own way.

Francisco Juan Cayuela (9)
Bridge & Patrixbourne CE Primary School, Canterbury

Untitled

It is amazing at first but it can cause pain.
It feels as magical as Disneyland.
It makes everyone smile.
It has a warm touch to it.
You would find you have it with your family and friends.
Everyone has it in their heart somewhere.

What am I?

Jessica Collins (8)
Bridge & Patrixbourne CE Primary School, Canterbury

Anger Is . . .

Anger is a dragon breathing fire on a hot day.
I hope it will be better tomorrow
With everyone happy and joyful.
Anger made all the other emotions run away.
Anger makes Nervous shiver and shake.
We all call Anger a big bully because he makes us cry.
I really don't like Anger when he gets out the wrong side of the bed.

Freddie Baker (9)
Bridge & Patrixbourne CE Primary School, Canterbury

What Am I?

I am gradually getting warmer and warmer by the minute.
I am in my bedroom stamping my feet.
Under the floor my mum is shouting, "Stop it!"
I am thinking of breaking a pencil.
I want to spend some time on my own.
I was shouting but my ears couldn't stand it any more.
What am I?

Oscar Nielsen Gorgojo (8)
Bridge & Patrixbourne CE Primary School, Canterbury

Guilt

When I feel guilt,
I just want to burst out with horror and confess.
When I feel guilt,
I get that build up of lies in my tummy
About to pop up and melt.
Guilt is that cloud of sadness bubbling up in your tummy
About to rain down with tears, making a puddle of pure misery.

Con Cussen (10)
Bridge & Patrixbourne CE Primary School, Canterbury

Rage

Rage lives in depths, deeper than anything.
Rage kicks off with screaming and then kicking.
Rage is a dart zooming through the dark red air.
Rage is an evil electric storm flashing through the sky.
Rage is a murky cave exploding at bedtime.
Rage is a bomb going *kaboom!*
Rage is a boiling pool of lava melting through vegetables.

Adam Chapman (9)
Bridge & Patrixbourne CE Primary School, Canterbury

Untitled

It is like the emotion 'like' but different
It is an emotion you will like
This happens to everyone
This includes boys and girls
This emotion is happy
Everybody likes this
What emotion am I?

William Green (7)
Bridge & Patrixbourne CE Primary School, Canterbury

Confusion

I make your eyes expand rapidly and
Your eyebrows shoot up like a jack-in-the-box.
I can slouch you and make you look a bit smaller.
I can sometimes make you wander around absent-mindedly,
Wondering what to do next, like a drunk elephant.
People look at me, making me feel embarrassed and angry.
What am I?

Wilfred Astin-Cooke (8)
Bridge & Patrixbourne CE Primary School, Canterbury

Excitement

When I'm excited I can't sleep
When I'm excited I count sheep
Excitement is a purring kitten
A race car going fast
A bomb going blast
When I get a toy
Excitement is joy.

Clayton Ferguson (9)
Bridge & Patrixbourne CE Primary School, Canterbury

Untitled

I make you warmer and warmer like the sun
I stomp my feet in my bedroom
Like a herd of elephants running down a hill
I might make you hurt someone
I am thinking of smashing a window
I shout so loud that it makes my ears pop
What am I?

Matthew McInally (8)
Bridge & Patrixbourne CE Primary School, Canterbury

Are You Nervous?

N ever goes away
E xciting, just annoys you
R ed is the colour you turn inside
V ery continuous, can't come when you want it
O pening its mouth, making your butterflies, let it all out
U ses it to stop you from doing what you want
S top it!

Charlotte Lucas (10)
Bridge & Patrixbourne CE Primary School, Canterbury

My Emotions

I feel joy when I get presents.
Joy is yellow like the buttercups in the field.

I feel sadness when someone hurts me on purpose.
Sadness is a dark puddle on the floor.

I feel guilt when I take something that is not mine.
Guilt is a funny feeling inside.

Amylee Norris (9)
Bridge & Patrixbourne CE Primary School, Canterbury

My Really Happy Feelings

Jumping up and down
Makes me smile
You might feel like this is Christmas
Feeling happy when it is your birthday
Usually I feel happy at Christmas
Or on a lovely summery day.

Ethan Hart (7)
Bridge & Patrixbourne CE Primary School, Canterbury

I'm Fury

I'm the thing that boils inside,
I'm the thing that never goes.
I'm the thing that you can't keep bottled,
I'm the thing that you can't escape.
I'm the thing that you have to beware of,
I'm the thing that you all fear.

Freya Hawkswell (10)
Bridge & Patrixbourne CE Primary School, Canterbury

My Emotions

I feel like I am going to explode with madness.
As cross as a bull.
When I am hungry, I am as bossy as can be.
When I lose I get furious.
When I get told off for nothing, I get very cross.
When someone calls me names, I get mad.

Adam McHale (8)
Bridge & Patrixbourne CE Primary School, Canterbury

Joyful

J oyful and happy
O verexcited and very glad
Y oung and cheery
F ull of excitement
U ndeterred in succeeding
L ooking good with joy.

Antoinette Sariev (10)
Bridge & Patrixbourne CE Primary School, Canterbury

My Emotion Is . . .

I can see but I normally cry.
I turn blue when I'm scared.
I cry as I'm a cloud.
I'm more shy than a mouse.
I begin with S and end with D.
What am I?

Jodi Hughes (7)
Bridge & Patrixbourne CE Primary School, Canterbury

Untitled

I never feel failure.
I always think positive that I can win.
I walk thoughtfully, constantly holding my head.
I hope for you in a winning way.
I help you do things you didn't know you could.
What am I?

Stanley DiBiase (8)
Bridge & Patrixbourne CE Primary School, Canterbury

Untitled

I hid under the table
Hoping that all the anger would stop.
I didn't dare speak.
I was tired of all the shouting.
My ears couldn't take it any longer.
I had to cover them and creep out of the room.

Ralph Drew (8)
Bridge & Patrixbourne CE Primary School, Canterbury

Super Mad

When you are always mad.
I am noisy when I am angry.
When I am mad, sometimes my tummy gurgles.
Sometimes I get super mad because this is the worst emotion.
Red-hot anger and slime coming out of your ears.

Thomas Newell (7)
Bridge & Patrixbourne CE Primary School, Canterbury

What Feeling Am I?

A nger shoots out of me like a bullet
N asty thoughts make me more frustrated
G oogle makes me annoyed when it doesn't work
E verything's wrong
R acing heart in my body.

Savanna Truelock (8)
Bridge & Patrixbourne CE Primary School, Canterbury

Shock Poem

Shock is the dark red landscape of horror.
The blood in your body.
The monster in your bed.
Shock is the taste of tasty chocolate at Cadbury World.
Shock is the sound of your loud, beating heart.

Charles Michael Easton (9)
Bridge & Patrixbourne CE Primary School, Canterbury

What Am I?

I have a red face like fire
I mostly run away from scary things
I sometimes have an upside down head
I hide behind things so no one sees me
Please can you help me?

Frankie Joseph John Nicholl (9)
Bridge & Patrixbourne CE Primary School, Canterbury

Emotions

You feel me when I am at home
It's like the world is upside down
It's like the universe inside out
I'm like this nearly all the time
What am I?

Pierce Michael Theodosiou (7)
Bridge & Patrixbourne CE Primary School, Canterbury

Jealousy Is . . .

Jealousy hides in the deepest, darkest corners of the Earth
And leaps out when you least expect it.
Jealously is a burning, blazing fire inside of me.
Jealously is a universe of longing.
Jealousy is purple with envy and has thin, narrow eyes for glaring.

Neve Goodfellow (9)
Bridge & Patrixbourne CE Primary School, Canterbury

Happy

My feelings are excited when they let me play.
My body has lots of energy to run.
I am happy when it is my birthday.
I am excited when my friends let me go to their house to play and
have tea.

Brian Budha Magar (7)
Bridge & Patrixbourne CE Primary School, Canterbury

Happy

H is for happy
A is for achievement
P is for peace
P is for poems
Y is for you and me.

Jasmine Murphy (7)
Bridge & Patrixbourne CE Primary School, Canterbury

Excitement

When I'm excited I can't sleep.
When I'm excited I count sheep.
I'm excited on birthdays, Christmas and Mother's Day.
I'm excited to have friends and family all around me.
I'm excited.

Poppy Holness-Bridge (10)
Bridge & Patrixbourne CE Primary School, Canterbury

What Am I?

I am as mad as a hurt lion.
It's just not fair!
She has the best braid for her hair.
I'll thump my fist like a mad man.
Until I have what she has.

Carmel Franks (8)
Bridge & Patrixbourne CE Primary School, Canterbury

How I'm Feeling

When I am losing.
When I get hurt.
If I get blamed for something I have not done.
My face burns like it is on fire.

Kristian Arshinev (7)
Bridge & Patrixbourne CE Primary School, Canterbury

On Top Of The World

Happiness is so beautiful,
It's like rainbows and sunshine.
To do things we enjoy,
To be with people we love,
To feel on top of the world.

Happiness is so beautiful.
It's like the glistening stars at night.
The love we get from our families.
The joy we get from our friends.
To feel on top of the world.

Happiness is so beautiful.
It's like the summertime and butterflies.
To laugh and be happy.
To smile and feel content.
To feel on top of the world.

Happiness is so beautiful.
It's like having all your wishes come true.
Christmas and birthdays are special too.
God has made this all for us.
This is what it feels like to be on top of the world.

Abigail Russell (9)
Fleetdown Primary School, Dartford

Happy Racer

I'm starting in tenth.
We are starting.
The wind is blowing in my sight.
One light, two lights, three lights, four lights, five lights
And we're off.
I had a fantastic start.
I am now in seventh.
We are now five laps into the race.
I am so happy I am in fifth place.
Ten laps to go and I have caught up to the front group.
Past one, then two, now three.
I am now head to head with first.
I'm passing him on the straight.
I am now first!
I am the happiest in the world!
Five laps to go.
I am passing the checkered flag.
I have won!
This is the best day of my life.

Benjamin Witham (8)
Fleetdown Primary School, Dartford

Joyfulness

The parties, the discos, full of fun and laughter.
Prizes and rewards, all shouting, 'Yay!'
Jokes and presents, everyone shouting, 'Wow, wee, ah!'
Time travelling, on a journey to a faraway land
With joyfulness everywhere and dolphins to celebrate.
Feel your joyfulness in your head.
Celebrate Christmas, birthdays, Easter
With chocolate, toys, money, cards and eggs.
Joy is fun, also giving you a spark in your head.
It gives us a good life and it is a gift from God.

Anna Yeldo (8)
Fleetdown Primary School, Dartford

Happy

I am always happy.
Ever since I was in a nappy.
I smile when I cuddle a bear.
I love it when I am at a fair.
I laugh at my funny, friendly friends,
They always make me happy.
I am always happy,
When I lose a tooth and I am gappy.
I smile when I eat my food,
I love it when I am in a happy mood.
I laugh at my super sister, Sophie,
She always makes me happy.
I am always happy.
I smile when I get a cuddle from my mummy.
I love it when my dinner is yummy.
I laugh at my fantastic, fabulous family.
They always make me happy.

Emma Fowler (8)
Fleetdown Primary School, Dartford

Angry Anger

Anger is a sign of red, as red as a tomato,
When I'm angry it makes me sad and naughty
Like a bored clown, also I'm wanting privacy because I'm annoyed.

Anger is as hot as a 1,000 chillies on fire
And as vicious as an alien.

I don't like it when people take stuff off me
And that makes me angry as a smashed glass
On the hard floor.

When I'm angry I feel embarrassed
Because I can't hold it in like a monkey
That can't climb a tree.

Rory Andrew Sargent (8)
Fleetdown Primary School, Dartford

Aggressive Anger

Anger is something that can change the whole day.
Anger sometimes goes the wrong way.
Whether it's a *Crash! Bang!* or *Yell!*
Anger can make things not go well,
Which way you choose, Anger sometimes may be there.
So enjoy the times you have to spare.
Anger is powerful and can worry your friends,
So be careful what you do, it can create problems.

Controlling Anger is sometimes confusing,
A good tip is to think of something amusing.
This will distract your stressed mind
And turn you into someone kind.
Anger is disobedient and doesn't follow the rules
And also occurs in schools.
This is why I have written this poem,
To help you with Anger. Now I'd best be going.

Rhianna Burford (8)
Fleetdown Primary School, Dartford

Leaving Bear

When I leave my dog I feel sad,
Even when I go to the shops
With my nan and grandad.

He will be home all on his own
With no one to talk to except for his bone.

I *whizz* round the shops so fast. I almost fall,
Even treat Bear to a brand new ball.
When I get home, I race through the door
And Bear is there waiting on the floor.

We have kisses and hugs,
I've missed him a lot
And I tickle him in his favourite spot!

Charlie Joseph Gilmore (8)
Fleetdown Primary School, Dartford

What Is Anger?

Sometimes I feel so angry,
I want to yell and scream
And wake up from this horrible dream.

I want to throw things,
Lie down, pound and flail,
Rant, rave and tantrum,
Deafen the world with my wail.

If I stage this fierce rebellion,
Will you return to me
To calm my broken heart?
Oh, how I want this possibility.

Anger won't bring you back,
But it's okay to express and feel,
Expressing the emotion of grief,
All of them help us to heal.

Grace Hunt (8)
Fleetdown Primary School, Dartford

My Happy Day

I wake up in the morning,
The sun is shining bright,
I jump out of bed, get dressed,
Then go to the park and fly my kite.

Lots of people have happy hearts,
While playing with their friends,
Smiling, laughing and joking around,
They never want the day to end.

A little treat to end the day
With a soft ice cream,
I had mine with a chocolate flake,
It tasted like a dream.

Kadey Turner (8)
Fleetdown Primary School, Dartford

Imagine A Day

Imagine a no school day,
A day of watching TV and having no homework.
Imagine meeting Lionel Messi in person.
Imagine a day doing no chores.
Just imagine a day eating KFC all day.
Imagine winning the lottery and getting £250,000 from it.
Imagine buying all the games in the game shop and getting FIFA 16.
Imagine buying a limousine, how would you feel?
Imagine your birthday was every day,
How many presents do you think you would get?
Imagine buying an Xbox One Live.
Imagine a day of respect and honesty.
Imagine being King or Queen of the world for a day,
Wouldn't that be awesome?
Imagine a day of kindness and everlasting smiles.
What kind of day did you imagine?

Oluwatise Alao-Adejumo (9)
Fleetdown Primary School, Dartford

The Love Poem

I lie on the ground
And stare into space,
The stars start to move
Into the shape of your face.

I see you there now,
Looking down at me,
With that cute little smile
That I like to see.

You say, 'Close your eyes,
Tell me what you see.'
I see two people,
Just you and me.

Bonnie Page (8)
Fleetdown Primary School, Dartford

The Frown That Makes You Sad

That frown on somebody's face that makes you sad,
It feels like you are going to melt,
Like chocolate melts when it is warmed up.
It makes you frown inside.
It makes you tremble like a city collapsing.
It makes you crumble like apple crumble in your kitchen oven.
Sad is the emotion that people hate to see on other people's faces
And I know that sad is my worst emotion of all.
I hope it is yours too.
Sad is something that I don't like to see on anybody's face.
I hate it with all my might.
Sad is like a gun pointed at somebody's head.
It's like a mother giving birth to a baby girl
And then the next thing you know,
The baby girl's lying in her mother's arms dead and not alive.

Emmanuel Edward (9)
Fleetdown Primary School, Dartford

My Poem Is About Happiness!

I
have what
it takes to
make people
happy. Happiness
Uplifts me and fills my
heart, mind and my soul.
Happiness gives me a sense of
relief, happiness warms my heart
and soul each day. Happiness can
Be seen in my eyes and smiles when I am
With my friends. I wake up each beautiful morning
With a bright smile to start each day.

Ayo Israel Babatunde (8)
Fleetdown Primary School, Dartford

I Feel Joy

I feel joy when I play football,
Especially when I score goals.

I feel joy when I watch my favourite film,
The one with the funny trolls.

I feel joy when I go bowling,
Always trying to get a strike.

I feel joy when we have days out,
Especially if I get to take my bike.

I feel joy when I am with my family,
They always make me laugh!

I feel joy at the end of a long day,
When I get to have a long bubble bath.

Evie Collins (8)
Fleetdown Primary School, Dartford

Swimming In Spain

Once my family went to Spain.
We found our perfect room so we stayed there.
We had so much fun at the water park
Using the slides and spying on Mum.

But best of all was the swimming pool
With very warm water
But it could be hotter.

Swimming and splashing made me feel happy.
I had a smile on my face while playing my best.
Jumping and diving was great fun
But doing flips was my best thing.
Soon we went home, ready for school
And I really missed my favourite swimming pool.

Amelia Kepa (8)
Fleetdown Primary School, Dartford

True Happiness

I am a happy person,
With several trophies won
That people like to see,
But they'll have to pay a fee.

I like to play at the park,
But the dogs always bark,
That people in the car,
Put their dogs a bit far.

Everyone should live happily
And they should live peacefully.
People should not be fighting,
But they should be smiling.

Akshat Kashyap (8)
Fleetdown Primary School, Dartford

Emotions Make Me Feel?

Emotions make me happy
They also make me sad
They also make me angry
And sometimes really mad.

Emotions make me feel disgust
They also make me fear
They also make me joyful
When my family is near.

But, happy is my favourite
Because it makes me feel
Amazing, super, awesome
Fantastic and so unreal.

Jack O'Brien (10)
Fleetdown Primary School, Dartford

Happiness

I feel happy when I open my Christmas present,
It can feel very pleasant.
I feel joyful on my birthday,
It's my special day!

I feel cheerful when I play a football match,
I am goalie and I can catch.
When I score, I go hardcore.

I feel happy when I go on the train,
It can be a little plain.
I am happy when I am on the bus,
There is lots of fuss.

Kodi Nwegbu (7)
Fleetdown Primary School, Dartford

Disgusting Times (Ewww!)

Disgusting times are gross!
You try to get your mind off it but you just can't.
This is a poem I am going to tell . . .
I was at home playing with my dolls.
Suddenly, my little brother was throwing up non-stop
Like he was spinning round non-stop.
In my head I was singing.
Eww, eww, eww, he is so gross. Eww!
Then I started throwing up, so then I was singing,
Eww, eww, eww! I am so gross!
I was so embarrassed, I was in tears!

Charissa Olabowale (7)
Fleetdown Primary School, Dartford

What Makes Me Happy!

Happiness is when a friend comes to tea
Or splashing about in the big, blue sea
Climbing high in a tall, green tree
And relaxing at home watching TV
That's what makes me happy
Cuddling my mum makes me smile
And playing on my Xbox for a while
Riding my bike for over a mile
Or wrestling my dog like a crocodile
That's what makes me happy.

Alex Taylor (8)
Fleetdown Primary School, Dartford

What Is Anger?

Anger is a firework about to go *whizz!*
It is like a powerful volcano ready to erupt,
It is rage when you're about to explode
Or when someone annoys you.
It makes you want to shout as loud as a fire alarm.
It wants you to charge like a raging rhinoceros.
It's a balloon about to *pop!*
Anger is a saucepan about to boil over.

All this makes you feel sorry afterwards.

Mason Howard (8)
Fleetdown Primary School, Dartford

Fear!

Fear is bad
Fear makes me sad
Fear makes everyone mad
It is like a pitch-black cave
I try to be brave
But bad boy Billy jumped out at me
It was so dark I could not see
In the end I tried my best
I found my way out and got some rest.

Finlay Robert Graham
Fleetdown Primary School, Dartford

Summer Fun!

Holidays are coming as clear as the sun,
The joy of six weeks off, away from the humdrum.
A smile is upon my face,
The sights and sounds of summer.
Playing out till late, it's just so great,
With my mates, all their toys from balls to tools.
Some special days I will always remember,
With family and friends from August to September.
Beach balls and buckets and no one to remember.

Gracie Rose Daniels (8)
Fleetdown Primary School, Dartford

Happiness

Music makes me happy,
It makes me jump for joy.
Money makes me happy,
I can buy a toy.
My family makes me happy,
They make me laugh so hard.
My family are so nice,
They make me take a bath.

Delsie Oluwatofarati Odulaja (8)
Fleetdown Primary School, Dartford

The Hot Emotion!

I sometimes get all het up when things don't go my way.
What really makes me angry is when I'm not allowed to play.
I hate it when I get told off for things I have not done,
So why don't all you grown-ups give me, Freya, some fun?
When I get told off, I get all hot and bothered,
I start to sweat, my face goes red,
And then I usually end up in bed.
Thanks Mum!

Freya Daniels (8)
Fleetdown Primary School, Dartford

Happy And Excited

When I go on a plane, it makes me happy
And when I'm happy it makes me smile.
When I smile, my eyes light up.
When I'm excited I start to jump up.
When I jump fast, being fast makes me blast.
But then I board an aeroplane
I know that it is true.

Lennon Donald Openshaw (8)
Fleetdown Primary School, Dartford

Sadness

I feel the sadness creeping in
Taking all the happiness out through my skin
It is so strong, I cannot stop
The sad thoughts that begin
I let them take over me
I cannot stop the tears from tumbling
I wish the sad thoughts would disappear
And let me just be me!

Sophie Louise Walton (8)
Fleetdown Primary School, Dartford

Happiness

Happiness is a sun in your heart
Happiness is as green as a leaf
Happiness can make you hyper
Instead of changing your baby's diaper
It will put wonders in your brain
It'll place a smiley face on your head
It burns worries away
So that they never come back again.

Feranmi Dere (8)
Fleetdown Primary School, Dartford

Solitary Times

S adness crawls over you when you feel alone
A n icy chill chokes your heart like a snake
D ark clouds drift above your head
N ow sadness is you . . .
E ating away your happiness
S olitary times
S olitary times.

Sean Robinson (7)
Fleetdown Primary School, Dartford

Happiness

Swimming makes me happy,
I feel like I'm floating in mid-air.
Underneath my swimming cap,
I keep my plaited hair.
The water is as warm as a sunny day,
It's like a spring day in May.

Neve Ripley Graham
Fleetdown Primary School, Dartford

Happiness

Happiness is when you're feeling good.
As good as a happy rabbit.
Happiness is when you're doing good stuff.
Happiness is when you're joyful and fantastic.
Happiness is when you're overjoyed, pleased,
Jolly, jubilant and cheerful.

Tyrell Loader (8)
Fleetdown Primary School, Dartford

Happy Summer Sun

S uper sunshine hits my face
U nstoppable beams of light
M agnificent views of summer sun
M agical summer breeze
E arth turns so we can see a sunrise
R ivers look as if they run into light.

Raiyah Gill (8)
Fleetdown Primary School, Dartford

Happiness

H appy teachers make children smile
A pologising makes teachers happy
P olite children make teachers happy
P eaches people eat happily
Y oung children are as happy as the sun.

Lewis Lam (9)
Fleetdown Primary School, Dartford

Anger

A nger makes me think of the colour red
N ever a happy feeling
G roan is what I do when I'm angry
E xcited is a million miles away from anger
R ed is the colour of your face when you're angry.

Natasha Sayer (8)
Fleetdown Primary School, Dartford

My Birthday Surprise

I'm so excited, I'm filled with joy,
I get to play with my new toy.
My cheeks are hurting, I'm smiling with glee,
Won't you come and play with me.

The candles get lit,
We all stand in line,
I give them a blow,
Then I realise it's time.

Because all my friends,
Have come to play,
I know it is,
My birthday!

Rachael Chance (8)
High Firs Primary School, Swanley

My First Goal

Today I scored my first goal
My teammate set me up
I passed to him and ran along
He passed back to me, it would never go wrong.

Today I scored my first goal
It felt so good, I was so excited
The joy I felt
And my mum was very delighted.

Today I scored my first goal
When I kicked the ball and scored
With the clapping and cheering
The crowd just roared.

Today I scored my first goal
Everyone screamed for me
It felt so great
With a tap on the back from my best mate.

Today I scored my first goal
Everyone was pleased for me, I felt tremendous
With the ball at the back of the net
Knowing that goal was glorious.

Today I scored my first goal
In the air the ball soared
Towards the net
And I just scored!

Today I scored my first goal
My dad was proud of me
He gave me a hug, ruffled my hair
In me a little footballer he could see.

Charlie Alexander Minter (8)
High Firs Primary School, Swanley

A World Of Happiness

Kicking leaves in the breeze
A rainbow carpet of leaves
A funny book I read
Made me laugh before going to bed
Funny pictures in the book
Why don't you take a look
At the funfair
Noise and madness in the air
Rides spinning round and round and upside down
I thought I would never touch the ground
Playing hide-and-seek with my cat
I fooled him into thinking there was a rat
Toys dangling and tossing through the air
Sounding like a fair
This is what makes me happy and
Cheerful.

Safiya Muddun (7)
High Firs Primary School, Swanley

What If

What if my work blows out the window?
What if it doesn't flow?
What if I do too much work?
What if I forget my work?
What if I get something wrong
Or what if I get it all wrong?
What if I eat a poisoned apple?
What if I hold a poison pen?
I wish I could start again.

Jalena Li-Hutchins
High Firs Primary School, Swanley

Happy Birthday

B rilliant
I am 9 today
R acing around
T oday, today
H appy birthday!
D ancing around
A mazing fun
Y ippee!

Ella Chance (8)
High Firs Primary School, Swanley

Hungry Pirates

P irates
I n the freezing cold
R eally hungry
A nd looking for their tea
T aste the smell of fish
E ating it in the chilling Arctic breeze
S miles and happiness when they see land.

Emily Chloe Burke (8)
High Firs Primary School, Swanley

Silly Sisters Laughing In The Sun!

S ometimes I'm silly with my sisters
I love to be silly on Saturdays
L ucy loves sizzling sausages and is silly
L aughter, loves and smiles
Y ellow sun delivers warm smiles.

Jessica Ellis (9)
High Firs Primary School, Swanley

Come Take A Walk

Today I'll walk in someone's shoes
Who will I pick, who will I choose?
Will they be nice, will they be glad,
Will they be mean, will they be sad?

The person I see is so full of glee
The light on her face shows all of her grace
So jubilant and full of merriment
Every minute with her is a joyous event.

This is the surface of her soul
Will the rest be as black as coal?

Today I'll walk farther in this girl's shoes
It's now more miserable and full of blues
Lamented she shows lots of tears
So depressed by all of her so-called peers.

This is another portion of her soul
It's gradually getting as black as coal.

Today I'll walk even further in this girl's shoes
She's feeling nauseous awaiting her next bruise
Timid and shy, how does she make it alright?
Frightened and scared, she soon has to fight.

This is the next section of her soul
It seems even darker than a piece of coal.

Today I'll walk even deeper in this girl's shoes
Her disgust in others, what does she have to lose?
The frustration and rage are building so high
Full of hatred and revenge, she wants to cry.

This is the final step into her soul
As dark as night and blacker than coal.

Today I'll walk to the end in this girl's shoes
So full of resilience, her temper she manages to diffuse.
A heart so brimming with bravery and honour
She is a warrior set free, so full of valour.

This is everything bared of her soul
Some parts as dark or darker than coal
But in the end she reached her goal
To see her life and have control.

Guess who I picked, guess who I chose?
The person I picked, for years I have known
These emotions and feeling all locked up inside
But now I know I no longer have to hide
These terrible times are all far behind.

Holly Keane
Hythe Bay CE Primary School, Hythe

Halloween

Spooky spiders and
Candle lighting,
Our bags full of sweets,
Really feel frightened,
In case you are a *witch!*

Ruby Papper
Kent College Junior School, Canterbury

Joy And Games

H olidays in China make me happy, always eating ice cream
A t the beach making amazing sand castles
P arks are so sunny, making me joyful
P arties make me smile
Y es, my life is all fun and games.

Qi-Chi Ella Ukpai (7)
Kent College Junior School, Canterbury

Read My Thoughts

I was about to step on stage
I was sweating
I was shaking
I felt dizzy
So I was tumbling about
I was about to faint . . .

How was I feeling?
Nervous.

Tilly Corteen-Coleman (8)
Kent College Junior School, Canterbury

Best Day Ever

B reakfast in bed
I ce cream at the park
R acing on the hill with my friends
T alking to my family
H ot cross buns for breakfast
D addy makes a special lunch
A t the table there's a birthday cake
Y awning with tiredness, I went to sleep.

Margot Gabriella Ali (7)
Kent College Junior School, Canterbury

Happy Thoughts

Eating sweets makes me happy.
Riding my pony makes me jolly.
Playing with my friends makes me joyful.
Going to see my nan's dogs make me feel fantastic.
Digging on a sandy beach makes me lovely.
Having fun with my cousins makes me smile.

Alexis Chaney (7)
Kent College Junior School, Canterbury

Hot Chocolate And Normal Chocolate

Hot chocolate makes me happy
When I taste it, it makes me warm
When I touch it, it makes me feel messy
When I smell it, it makes me feel excited
I don't like white chocolate or dark, it makes me poorly
I would open the chocolate slowly
Because I feel worried and nervous
That I won't get the golden ticket
Chocolate is from Ghana in Africa
It is far away
I don't care if it's far away
I live in England, it makes me happy.

Georgina Fraher (9)
Meadowfield School, Sittingbourne

Chocolate

Chocolate makes me feel good.
When I eat I'm happy.
Dark chocolate is my favourite.
Hot chocolate makes me feel nice.
Hot chocolate makes me feel warm inside.
I want to win a golden ticket.
It makes me feel excited.
I don't like white chocolate
It makes me feel sick.

Alec Kane (8)
Meadowfield School, Sittingbourne

The Foxes White Chocolate Factory

Mmmm, I love chocolate, it makes me feel happy.
Dark chocolate makes me feel poorly and sick.
When I taste milk chocolate, it makes me feel excited.
I feel lovely when I smell white chocolate.
White chocolate makes me feel sick in my mouth.
When I get a golden ticket I will feel proud.
I am scared about the chocolate factory.

Gemma Law (8), Taylor Reading & James Wallis (10)
Meadowfield School, Sittingbourne

Chocolate

Chocolate is beautiful
It melts in my mouth
Chocolate feels nice
Dark chocolate - love it
White chocolate - love it
Going down my throat
I dream about chocolate
Chocolate is delicious.

Guy Worthington
Meadowfield School, Sittingbourne

Chocolate

Chocolate is beautiful
It melts in my mouth
Chocolate feels nice
Dark chocolate - love it
White chocolate - love it
Going down my throat
I dream about chocolate
Chocolate is delicious.

Luke Powney (10)
Meadowfield School, Sittingbourne

Chocolate

I am starving when I see milk chocolate.
Black chocolate tastes yucky.
Hot chocolate is delicious.
White chocolate makes me feel happy.
When I won the golden ticket I was excited.

Ewan Patrick Ayers (8)
Meadowfield School, Sittingbourne

Not The White Chocolate

Milk chocolate makes me feel hungry.
White chocolate smells yucky.
Dark chocolate feels nice in my mouth.
Hot chocolate is warm in my tummy.

Kai Cumberland (9)
Meadowfield School, Sittingbourne

Days Of The Week

Monday is the first day of the week,
I've already made friends with Zoe and Zeke.
Happy is my favourite emotion,
I just hope I don't end up in the ocean!

Help! Help! Tuesday already,
One of the worst in the week.
I fell over first and now lost my teddy,
How could it get worse, I'm a freak.

Wednesday has come, Tuesday is over,
Though I shouldn't get too excited,
For all my friends made fun of me,
When they saw the cut on my knee.

Thursday has come, got into a fight,
Not so great as it was quite a fright.
What will happen if the teacher finds out,
I hope she doesn't!

Friday, Friday, last day of the week,
Well, that week wasn't so sleek.
Soon will be the weekend, hooray,
Then I'll have all my friends round to play.

Rachel Robertson (10)
Roseacre Junior School, Maidstone

Your Emotions

E nvy is worst
M isery also counts
O verjoyed I always am
T iredness causes crying
I rritated a lot by my brother
O verjoyed I still am
N ervous when I speak to the new teachers
S cared - well that's an emotion!

Molly Stuart (7)
Roseacre Junior School, Maidstone

Loveliness

When you're in love you usually see a dove
You're the love, I feel excited
The girl made me a bead necklace
The leaves are green but beautiful boy is never ever, ever mean
I feel like I'm starting to love him!

I feel like I'm going to explode with love
There's love, doves and also I have gloves!
I feel like I'm going to marry him, he's amazing
I love him, he's happy
I love his smile
I love you and also I think you love me
Let's celebrate with a roast and peas.

We love each other as much as I love Mummy
He loves me as much as doves love each other
I love him even more than dear future husband
(I love dear future husband)

I feel like I could kiss him but not a dustbin
I am feeling like I really love you (I'm really going to marry him).

Caitlin Baker (7)
Roseacre Junior School, Maidstone

Babies Are Happy

I think babies are always happy,
Because they have a cosy nappy,
Also because their food is pappy,
So babies are always happy.

B abies are happy,
A nd have nappies,
B ecause babies are happy I am,
I love pappy food,
E xcited because babies are happy
S o I am happy and so are babies!

Flora Gillies (7)
Roseacre Junior School, Maidstone

Big Fuss, The 11+

In my school there's a big fuss
It's over the Kent test or the 11+.

People who've passed,
People who've failed.
Some of them smiled,
Some of them wailed.

Giggling girls wanting to know,
What school will you choose?
Where will you go?

People who didn't pass could feel left out,
Don't understand what the fuss is about.

You're not suddenly better than me,
You'll still want me round for tea.

Mum and Dad laugh,
They find it quite funny
'You need to be savvy not clever
To make money.'

Cookie Rags Martin (10)
Roseacre Junior School, Maidstone

Christmas Is To Me . . . ?

Christmas is fun with lots of snow
Christmas is special with the family
Christmas is bright and colourful with the twinkling lights
Christmas is fun making and throwing snowballs and building
snowmen
Christmas is fun eating Christmas pudding
Christmas is exciting, listening to Christmas carols
Christmas is seeing Santa Claus and feeding his reindeer
Christmas is getting presents from Santa
Christmas is a fun time playing with all my new toys.

Haden Lines (8)
Roseacre Junior School, Maidstone

Fear Has Come To Play

It's that time again, the time I dread,
When scary thoughts fill my head.
Fear has come to play,
There's a man lurking under my bed,
A creepy doll with a broken head.
Fear has come to play.
Fear is knocking at my door,
Creeping, crawling across the floor.
Fear has come to play.
I wanted to scream, but my throat was tight,
The eerie sound in the dead of night.
Fear has come to play.
Fear crept into every corner - in my wardrobe, in my bed,
Filling dark thoughts in my head.
Fear has come to play.
Bear's bony fingers tap on my windowsill,
Whispering how he likes to kill.
Fear has come to play.

Ellie Pizzey (10)
Roseacre Junior School, Maidstone

It's My Go!

I was shivering, shivering as if I was in an ice bath.
My face was as red as a roaring fire and burning lava.
My mouth was as dry as a desert.
I had shrivelled up cheeks.
My memory was blank.
I was breathless.
My heart was thumping loudly.
I had visible goosebumps.
Suddenly, I gave a great ghastly gulp.
Everyone stared.
I could feel their eyes burning into my skin.

Ava Cudmore-Smith (8)
Roseacre Junior School, Maidstone

101

A Sad Ending

Dead, yes dead,
And in my quivering body my melting heart has gone to bed.
I felt as if someone had pulled the thumping red thing out of me.
I could feel noises vibrating,
My darling dog was gone.
I was practically glued to my chair.
The colossal lump in my throat made it almost impossible to breathe.
Although they say he has gone to a better place, I think not.
In my mind I imagine the poor little darling floating motionless
Through a swirling sea of sadness,
Like a fluffy white cat in a murky, grey pond.
You belong with me, not the fiery red souls that pull you apart.
My dear Max, I miss you so,
You left me too soon.
Now my heartbeat slows and I fear to join you,
Standing in a whispering world watching me worriedly.
Wherever you are you will always be in my heart.
I love you, Max.

Jessica Maisie Ryan (9)
Roseacre Junior School, Maidstone

The Happiness At Christmas Time

C ookies crumbling in my mouth
H eart pounding
R eindeer pouncing magically on the road
I ndoors being cosy and warm
S anta coming to give presents to everyone
T ears of joy
M ore, more presents for everyone
A nd last of all
S ome people coming around.

Molly Shellaker (10)
Roseacre Junior School, Maidstone

My Day At The Beach

The beach is my special place,
It has sand and shells and water,
I like it when the tide comes rolling in,
Building sand castles that glitter in the sun,
Fossil collecting and shell spotting are what I do best,
Jumping, diving, splashing,
Hitting the water and swimming to shore,
Dancing, daydreaming over the rocks,
Not aware of my surroundings,
Enjoying myself so much,
Sitting down in the sweltering sand,
Burying my dad whilst being smothered in suncream by my mum,
Playing football with my brother right next to the sea,
Rushing in from the ocean every time we kicked the ball,
At the end of the day my feet are sore and my fingers hurt.
That was my day at the beach
And when we got home, I was a sleeping lion.

Lucy Ann Hyland (10)
Roseacre Junior School, Maidstone

Getting Really Excited Watching Fireworks

It's exciting
Thinking about fireworks
Edging towards the night sky
In celebrations
Rockets rise in the sky
Exploding in beautiful colourful displays
They race
Over the heads of excited children
Wonderful rainbows bursting overhead
Near a garden shed.

Elleanor Robson (7)
Roseacre Junior School, Maidstone

Mean Old Anger

Anger is evil, anger is mean,
He'll moan at you day and night,
Even when he murmurs goodnight.
Shout! Shout! Groan! Groan!
He's rude, he's mean, he's horrid.
Nobody wants to be near.
He hits, he kicks, he punches, he shoves,
He definitely doesn't love.
Mean old anger.
He occurs here and he occurs there,
He occurs when your mum says 'No!'
He doesn't like you, he doesn't like me,
He doesn't like anyone much.
He will moan and he will groan,
But that's just how anger is.

Joseph Stone (8)
Roseacre Junior School, Maidstone

Disappointment

Disappointment is worse than anger,
Worse than any type of punishment,
You can ever think of.

Disappointment reaches out to your heart,
Makes you feel
You'll never reach the stars.

For some reason you're sad,
Yet nobody's mad,
You know how they feel
So you still share a meal.

You think to yourself,
I'll never be naughty again,
But they never told you off.

Neve Benson-Dare (9)
Roseacre Junior School, Maidstone

Fear He Is Here

Fear, he is here
He is scared, that's clear
He is scared of a butterfly
He is scared of a hat
When you look at him, he is even scared of that!

He screams when he watches a movie
He is frightened of a book
He is even scared to have a boogie
How frightened is that?

You would think he is scared enough, but that is not true
Like he is scared of drawing and even going to the loo!
He is even scared of flowers
So when someone brought them in, all he said was
"Chuck them in the bin!"

Lily Mace (7)
Roseacre Junior School, Maidstone

The Creature Teacher

On my first day of school,
The teacher was shouting like a mad creature.
I was so scared, I went as pale as a ghost.
The next day it was maths,
That teacher was shouting like a creature.
I was so scared, I fell off my chair.
This time I didn't just go as white as a ghost,
But I also went as white as tissue paper
I fell off my chair.
The teacher shouted at me.
I was so scared, I didn't know what to say.
At home I told my mum and dad about the teacher creature,
They were both horrified,
So I went to a different school.

Violet Robinson (8)
Roseacre Junior School, Maidstone

The Sadness Monster

The sadness monster came one day,
He crawled into my mind,
I would never have seen him,
He simply jumped in from behind.
He told me about my sister,
That her hair would fall off,
That she had cancer
And it would start with a cough.
I ordered the monster to go away,
But it shook its head and demanded to stay.
Then I got tearful and started to cry,
I really had had enough.
But then I felt brave and stood up to the monster
To prove he wasn't so tough.

Sienna Campbell (9)
Roseacre Junior School, Maidstone

A Roller Coaster Ride Of Emotion!

It bubbles up inside you like a cauldron,
And can disappear as rapidly as an eagle's swoop.
Adrenaline pumps through your body like a drum beat,
Your insides turn into a washing machine
As your feelings get churned repeatedly around.
Getting ever faster, ever closer,
The moment comes.
Suddenly, exhilaration evaporates,
Replaced by anxiety, fear and doubt.
Will I fall?
The nibble of the nails starts.
My turn is next!

Evie McKeon (10)
Roseacre Junior School, Maidstone

Excitement

I am as excited as ever,
It's my sister's second birthday.
One more sleep until the birthday fairy comes,
It is her special day!

Presents with paper as sparkly as can be,
Cake is so yummy.
We got her a new Pooh bear,
Who really likes honey!

What else will she get?
I really can't wait,
It is so exciting,
It is a very special day!

Leah Hammond (7)
Roseacre Junior School, Maidstone

Fantastic Food

Food, food everywhere,
Cakes, chocolate and sweets,
Are just a few of my favourite treats.

Raining marshmallows and hot chocolate rivers,
This is my dream,
I wish it would come true.

Chips are nice, burgers are yummy,
I like baked beans in my tummy.
Chicken, pasta, jacket potato and rice with cheese,
All these things sound really nice.

Which one to choose? Just cannot decide.

Chantelle Butler (8)
Roseacre Junior School, Maidstone

107

Joy

Joy, joy, joy, it's what dreams are all about.
Joy, joy, joy, you don't leave us with any doubt.
Joy, joy, joy, you are the best.
Joy, joy, joy, you shine like a golden treasure chest.
Joy, joy, joy, you're like a magical Christmas time.
Joy, joy, joy, you are certainly mighty fine.
Joy, joy, joy, always inside a person's soul.
Joy, joy, joy, making you feel whole.
Joy, joy, joy, you're brighter than the sun,
Joy, joy, joy, always bringing lots of fun.

Erin McGregor (8)
Roseacre Junior School, Maidstone

Happiness Around The World

H appy hippos swimming in the river
A round the world families are very happy
P enguins waddling on the snow
P eople singing and people dancing
I think we should all be happy
N o one should be sad, not even me!
E ngland - here we have lots of rain but we still smile
S miles on everyone's faces
S o everyone's happy and that's how it will stay.

Abigael T Miller (11)
Roseacre Junior School, Maidstone

My Happiness Poem

H earing the sound of the yummy ice cream van
A ward ceremonies where I win
P latefuls of fish and chips with plenty of ketchup
P laying laser quest with my friends
 I nteresting experiments on the BBQ
N utella pancakes with bananas
E nthusiastic jumps on the trampoline
S uper bubbly warm baths
S itting with my family and a warm cup of tea.

Matthew McKeon (7)
Roseacre Junior School, Maidstone

Exciting Holiday Moments

One sunny morning I woke up yawning,
I exploded with excitement at the dawning of a new day.
I felt bubbles bubbling up inside me for a new experience.
I could hardly contain my excitement, what a wonderful feeling.
Holidays!
Sun, sand, sea, and swimming,
These are the things I love seeing and doing.
This embodies my excitement.

Abbie Outram (9)
Roseacre Junior School, Maidstone

![YoungWriters]

Boredom

B rilliant brain block
O MG nothing to do
R ight, think
E mbrace the quiet sound of your heartbeat
D igging around in my pocket for something to do
O pen my eyes
M illie my dog, go play with her.

Lily Halpin (10)
Roseacre Junior School, Maidstone

What Happy Does

H appy is the best emotion ever
A ctive like a small puppy going for a walk
P resents make you happy, then you feel grateful
P ets feel happy when you play with them and give them love
Y ou always feel happy when you have fun.

Ashleigh Yates (10)
Roseacre Junior School, Maidstone

Anger

Anger is a fireball that bubbles up inside you,
It seems to come out at the most unexpected times.
It kicks, punches, bites and hits,
It seems to have a mind of its own.

Lily Crossley (9)
Roseacre Junior School, Maidstone

Stress

The fire wants to play,
He gets you angry,
He sets you alight,
With fumes.

You go crazy!
Your friends go zany,
You want to explode
With distress.
You agonise with stress,
Your face glows with fury.

He wants to punch,
So while you munch on your lunch,
He flicks and kicks
With all his might.

He bellows
And screams
With distress,
You punch
And kick.

Fumes and fire come from your ears,
Bombs drop,
Your eyes get bloodshot,
Your face goes red.

George Allen (9)
St Faith's At Ash Preparatory School, Canterbury

Anger

It battles,
It fights,
It swears,
It bites,
All day long.

It kills,
It rages,
It fills
Your tummy with anger.

Your brain goes all mushy,
You turn into destruction mode,
It takes a code,
To break the mean machine,
It's small, it's fat, it's lean,
It's cunning, it's sly,
It hurts you and me,
Till we cry.

Lenny Delo (9)
St Faith's At Ash Preparatory School, Canterbury

Sad Is Bad

S ad is horrible
A nxious and
D estroyed also

I ndestructible
S ad is bad

B eing angry? King of
A nd the worst of them all . . .
D estroyed my heart.

Joshua Bayliss (10)
St Faith's At Ash Preparatory School, Canterbury

Deadly Rage

A storm kicks through you,
You will scream and shout,
No matter how hard you try,
Sometimes you can't let it out.

He will run through your body,
Full of rage,
No matter how hard you try,
He won't die of age.

The lightning and thunder,
You make them fear,
No matter how hard you try,
He will always be near.

But after a while,
It starts to lack,
No matter how hard you try,
One day he will come back.

George Hunt (10)
St Faith's At Ash Preparatory School, Canterbury

Worrying

I'm lying here in my bed,
Bad thoughts are rushing through my head.
I just worry all the time,
Am I not doing well, am I being unkind?
What if a child-snatcher walked through my door
Shouting, 'You will be mine by the break of dawn.'
What if a potion came through a magical portal
And if I drank it, it would make me immortal.
Now that would be quite cool and fun,
But I'd test it out by walking on the sun!
All these worries and all these fears,
But now I'm cuddling with Mum, who's wiping away my tears.

Amelia Goddard (9)
St Faith's At Ash Preparatory School, Canterbury

113

Christmas

S tockings everywhere
A ll of us in comfy clothes
N ever say never
T eatime
A nother good year is coming up

I can see a bright future
S tar in the night sky

C hristmas is here!
O pening presents
M ummy in the kitchen cooking
I am very sleepy
N ight-time
G oodnight and have a brilliant Christmas.

Madeline Ford (9)
St Faith's At Ash Preparatory School, Canterbury

What To Do?

He's whispering in my ear,
Horrible things I don't want to hear.
He's coming closer to me,
I don't want to look and see.
I'm nervous, I'm nervous,
I'm sad, I'm sad,
I've all these emotions and it's really, really bad.
I'm not happy and flappy,
I'm droppy and whoopy.
Anger, fear,
Which one should I hear?
'Cause I'm scared and teared,
What shall I do?

Honor James (9)
St Faith's At Ash Preparatory School, Canterbury

Confusion

Confusion, a puzzle in your mind,
Confusion, a feeling worse than any kind.
Confusion, a time when you are in despair,
Confusion, a question like what to wear?

Confusion, when you just cannot think,
Confusion, when the answers just don't link.
Confusion, a horrible, horrible feeling,
But when you get the answer, your senses go reeling.

Leya Carter (9)
St Faith's At Ash Preparatory School, Canterbury

A Riddle

I am usually inside, on the side of the bed
I flop and stop
When I get to a bed I jump in it!
I look sad but I am angry inside
And I flop.
When I see a bed I stop to flop in it
And then I sleep and don't wake up for ages!

A: Tiredness

Dafna Aron (9)
St Faith's At Ash Preparatory School, Canterbury

Anger

Anger is a feeling that hides inside you
And when it is let loose,
Everyone is scared.
You don't know what to do,
But all you need is take a very deep breath
And then everything will be fine.
Anger will come again, but not for some time.

Madeline Read (9)
St Faith's At Ash Preparatory School, Canterbury

Anger

When I get cross and annoyed
I get angry and furious and all crazy inside
My eyes go red, my face goes purple
I go rumbling, tumbling and moody inside
My anger, it lives in the deepest, darkest place of all
I hate it when he bursts out all so . . . so . . . angry
He drives me mad and insane, I go bonkers and get baffled.

Barney Batchelor (9)
St Faith's At Ash Preparatory School, Canterbury

Disgust

D ainty, green fingers that push away greens
I ndigestion comes upon her like she's seen a portion of peas
S alty sea water makes her cough constantly
G loopy, yellow mustard gives her wind rapidly
U nsalted butter makes her projectile vomit
S he hates her fish with grey stuff, she says it looks quite rusty
T o be honest, she's a bit fussy.

Millie Rigden (9)
St Faith's At Ash Preparatory School, Canterbury

My Sadness Poem

S adness makes you cry inside
A nd everyone is shouting at you
D aniel doesn't like me
N o one else does
E veryone is saying sorry
S adness does make you sick inside
S adness is draining out like lemon juice coming out of a lemon.

Millie Fidock (9)
St Faith's At Ash Preparatory School, Canterbury

Hatred

H ate is a strong emotion
A ngry as a cornered lion
T ough as a hating mind
R ed as a pool of trickling blood
E arwigging in your kindness making an unstoppable tide of rage
D eafening rage coming to your ears, stopping the whispering voices of kindness.

Felix Edelman (9)
St Faith's At Ash Preparatory School, Canterbury

Happy

H appiness is a wonderful thing
A lways giggling and laughing
P eople having so much fun
P arty all around
Y es, happiness is a lovely thing that keeps everyone smiling.

Boo Cruwys (9)
St Faith's At Ash Preparatory School, Canterbury

Anger

I'm as angry as a bull at a red flag,
A bullet firing at me at the speed of light,
Sprinting away quicker than a lightning bolt,
I'm an angry, bloodsucking vampire,
I'm running as bloodthirsty as I've ever been.

Hayden Taylor-Worth (9)
St Faith's At Ash Preparatory School, Canterbury

The Amazing Feeling Of Joy

Joy bursts out and makes you smile,
Being angry is totally futile.
Jumping Joy can save the day,
In all the nice, mysterious ways.
Joy is like a speck of sun
And you'll do a rapid run.
Try to keep it for a week,
You'll be a tall mountain peak.
Finding love and joy to seek,
Let any anger go out like a leak.
When you feel this amazing way,
Just remember, don't change today.
When this amazing feeling's done,
Try to manage a joyous hum.

Carla Spooner (9)
St Stephen's Primary School, Tonbridge

Sadness

I'm alone in class
Drooping down like a dead flower
My eyes are gushing like a river
Sadness is not a great feeling
My smile has dropped and turned to a frown
Life is hard when you're sad
My hands are shaking
I'm beginning to turn to ice
My face is turning blue
There's a lump in my throat!

Paris Watson (9)
St Stephen's Primary School, Tonbridge

Happy

When I am happy
The flowers awake
The birds are flappy
The sun shines during the day
That's what makes me happy
Happy is always following me, every which way
At night when I'm happy
Stars are twinkling in the sky
The moon is up and saying hi.

Keira-Sienna Simpson (9)
St Stephen's Primary School, Tonbridge

Anger Of You!

Anger bursts out at you, like a roaring lion.
It pushes and pulls and it makes you really violent.
Anger makes you bark like a pet.
It makes you mad and very, very sad.

People get angry, they're not glad,
People get angry and very sad.
So throw it in the trash
With a big, bad bash.

Josh Fox Cousins (9)
St Stephen's Primary School, Tonbridge

Anger

Anger was like a fireball across the sky
It lives deep in your heart
It can control you and hurt your friend
The anger only runs away if you take a deep breath
Your nose - out comes steam!
My body was being punched
Now I sleep, I'm still angry
And now we will be angry forever!

Guopeng Wu (9)
St Stephen's Primary School, Tonbridge

Anger!

Anger is a fiery, bulging ball of red gas inside your body.
Put it back in its wooden box.
Anger shouts, 'Bye!' as it escapes its way out.
Anger is futile, pointless.
Cheer yourself up and throw it away in the trash.
Anger is a terrible feeling, you need the best feeling.
Don't be angry!

Alfie Sims (9)
St Stephen's Primary School, Tonbridge

The Happy Poem

H aving this emotion is the key to life
A power to be able to make friends
P eople respect others with this emotion
P retend to possess this emotion and you will go nowhere
Y ou should be proud to own this emotion.

Jonny Hosier (10)
St Stephen's Primary School, Tonbridge

The Power Of Happiness

When you wake up in the morning,
When the day is still dawning,
Sunshine soaring into the sky,
I straighten out my tie,
And I truly feel amazing,
Whilst the cheerful cows are grazing,
And I want to ride the sun,
Whilst eating a cream bun,
The warmth heats up my heart today,
Everything is awesome, hooray!
Now it's time to see,
Where I can be,
In this outstanding morning with you.

Ethan Louis Clarke (10)
Scotts Park Primary School, Bromley

Anger!

Anger churning in my head,
Quickly, quickly, going red.
Fists are curling, tears are burning,
Everything just seems to stop.

Fires starting in my mind,
Feels like an apocalypse.
The world looks like a blurry haze,
It has no end, I'm in a maze!

Everything has been forgotten,
As the wind blows in my face.
Time has stopped, I feel no better,
I am angry, that is that!

Alexandra Cioran (11)
Scotts Park Primary School, Bromley

Sigh . . .

Hi, I'm me; plain old me,
Doubtful Disgust, that's who I am.
Sigh . . .
No one likes me,
I'm nobody's man.

I'm just the annoying girl of disgusting emotion,
I'm just a sludge of marshy green.
Sigh . . .
I feel so strange,
I feel so . . . mean.

My mother; she's trust and as cream as can be,
My father is excitement; the gold of the sun.
Sigh . . . I'm green, plain green.
My brother . . . surprise, so mellow, but why?

My sister's so joyful, she's yellow and fun.
Sigh . . .

Now, meet the rest of my family.
My dog called Snoopy - turquoise and afraid.
Sigh . . . he's so cute!
My grandma, always weeping; a shade of mint green,
My grandad - dark green and angry, but that's the way we were
made.

We are the cabbages, the leeks, the onions and tomatoes,
We are the worms, the beetles, the slugs and the snails.
We're down in the dirt and kicked in the face,
They're the sweet things, the chocolate, the beautiful whales.

But why?
Sigh . . .

Elodie Stephens (9)
Southborough CE Primary School, Tunbridge Wells

There's A Girl I Despise

Over there, there's a girl
I despise, she lies.
She has all the friends in the world,
She is King of her pride.
Every PE lesson she is on top,
I think it should stop!
She once tattled on me for stealing a nest,
Yet she didn't tattle on the rest.
Her parents say she's the apple of their eye,
Where as my parents just look and sigh.
She always has the top spot,
On the teacher's board,
When I am down upon the ground,
Stuck with the ones that cry.
Her hair is beautifully plaited,
And mine is terribly matted.
She is a winner - best in class,
Whilst I just come dead last.

Sophie Hannah Barden (9)
Southborough CE Primary School, Tunbridge Wells

Fear

In the most malevolent places, fear lurks,
It threatens and it terrorises whenever you step into trouble,
Often triggered by its close comrade,
The chaotic and horrific panic; hyena of emotions.

Whether you are in shadowy caves, the sinister poltergeists haunt,
Or where the grisly gravestones skulk,
Fear can strike in the place one despises the most, like a despicable
cobra.
Only when an hospitable, amiable force materialises,
The invidious fiend named Fear is subdued.

Yuqi Pan (10)
Warren Road Primary School, Orpington

If Only, If Only - Depression

Depression
It's a place,
A place you can't escape.
Locked in a cell,
Deep inside your head.
Looking for help?
Well, it's not there.

If only, if only,
They saw the suffering you've been through.

You feel like running away from yourself,
As if somebody is taking over your thinking,
Who could this be?
Your shoulders feel tight but you hold the pain in every day.

If only, if only,
A day will come when the bright sun
Will wash away all the darkness of *our* lives.

Yes, I know just how you're feeling.
Day after day, I put on my mask,
Happy, cheerful, and possess no worries.
That is what everyone around me also thinks,
That I am a happy, fearless girl, but on the inside I'm not.

If only, if only,
They knew how the slow and painful torture kills all contentment.

I feel dejected when I'm alone and very miserable.
Sometimes those grey thoughts come to mind;
Detained in living hell with the Devil,
I'm glad to know that I'm not the only one with an everyday mask.
Nevertheless you can do the right thing.
Leave with a fight . . .

Nicole Onyia (10)
Warren Road Primary School, Orpington

Losing Her

My heart thumps in my chest,
She smiles at me for what could be the last time;
I clutch her shaky hand,
And gulp with misery.
My heart thumps in my chest,
I sit cautiously down on the comforting bed;
The thought of losing her,
Is just too much to bear.

My heart thumps in my chest,
Tears prick my eyes, but I try to stay strong for her;
Her wrinkled face is calm,
But I am in despair.
My heart thumps in my chest,
The time is drawing closer to say my goodbyes;
I will miss her so much,
I'll never forget her.

Her hand grips my palm,
Her eyes stare into darkness;
She takes one last breath,
Her heart is dying,
Her life is ending.
My heart thumps in my chest,
Her pain has ceased, but mine is just beginning;
Without her,

I am lost . . .

Lucy Carr (10)
Warren Road Primary School, Orpington

Lost

Boom, boom, boom.
My uneasy heart pumps under my soaked T-shirt.
Anxiety fills my soul, squeezing through my veins.
Could someone possibly help me?

Boom, boom, boom.
My eyesight turns hazy
As I look down at my trembling, clammy hands.
Will I stay like this forever?

Boom, boom, boom.
Dark clouds fill my panicked, worried mind.
Anticipating my fate, I wonder if I'll ever see her again.
People dash past, could one of them be her?

Boom, boom, boom.
Sickly, sweet smell of candyfloss envelops my nostrils,
Making my stomach feel even more sick.
Will I be able to munch this sugary goodness with her again?

Boom, boom, boom.
Even though there are masses of people, I feel lonely,
Lonely without her.
I am lost.

Kirsty Rose Hunt (11)
Warren Road Primary School, Orpington

Anger

Sometimes I want to shout and scream
And lock myself inside.
Sometimes I want to let it out
And want to run and hide.

Don't tell me that you understand
Because I know you don't!
Don't tell me that you'll help me out
Because I know you won't.

I'll slam stuff on the table
I'll throw stuff on the floor
But only to prove my point
That you prefer me
When I'm behind a heavy door.

Accept me in my ups and downs
Because this is just me
Accept me in my quirkiness
I am who I am!

Helena Cvjetan (10)
Warren Road Primary School, Orpington

Anger

I can feel it building up inside me,
Then suddenly it bursts out
And now everyone can see
That anger is taking over me!

The hidden storm is a speeding bullet,
I start raging and ranting,
The infuriation is now at its fullest,
Because, anger is taking over me!

Now it is at its highest,
I try to start to stop it,
For even my mouth is at its driest,
Because, anger is taking over me!

My heart is pounding like a drum,
As anger has an outburst,
Everybody can see I am glum,
Anger has taken all of me!

Anika Tibrewal (10)
Warren Road Primary School, Orpington

Fear Of The Door

Slowly turn and face the door,
Just put your hand out and grasp the handle,
But the darkness that taunts you best,
It'll plant terror in your hearts.

An awful image drifts in front of my eyes,
I scream. My heart beats faster, adrenaline pumping;
The fear that hides in deep, dark shadows,
The monster that murders your soul, that takes over.

My heart thumps.
A lump stuck in my throat.
I wish a hole would swallow me up,
Making me smaller, smaller, smaller.

I put my palms on the handle,
Tiny hands restrain me from turning.
I surge forward and shake off the hands;
I open the door.

Nana Beney (10)
Warren Road Primary School, Orpington

The Wander

Thoughts swirled round me, like a merciless hurricane;
The tranquil surroundings soothed my soul,
As my cares slowly drifted away.
A silent atmosphere coated the area around me,
An uncomfortable feeling spread rapidly through my bones.
Its dark eyes watched from a distance,
Crystal-coloured beams of electricity splintered the midnight sky.

The surrounding area was engulfed by a sudden shard of deadly
light.
I heard the darkness cackling, watching me cower in fear of the
storm,
The darkness reached out . . .

Dillon Precious (10)
Warren Road Primary School, Orpington

Anger

Roaring, screeching, bellowing,
Everyone has it,
It burns within us,
And kills contentment on its way.

Howling, clamouring, shrieking,
Demolishes delight everywhere,
Annihilating everything,
Like dynamite, it ravages everyone.

Whining, hollering, growling,
Uncontrollably bursts into a tantrum,
Torture is its middle name,
Abusing the world around it.

Silent, calm, gone,
Now only a little flame,
Incarcerated deep inside us.

Mlak Elbuzidi (10)
Warren Road Primary School, Orpington

Sadness

It hides in the shadows, staying out of sight,
It whimpers in the darkness, without much might,
But when it comes out, it can make you shocked,
People might knock, but the door will stay locked.

When it leaps out it can make you cry,
And people stop and stare, as they walk by.
Sometimes, it drowns you in a sea of despair,
You could look for happiness, but it would not be there.

You might think you're scared, but you might be sad too,
You might just not know and that can be true.
Sometimes it comes in a grey cloak of gloom,
But sometimes it stays in the hopelessness room.

James Moulden (11)
Warren Road Primary School, Orpington

Anger

Anger,
He dwells inside my head,
Creeping up every now and then.
I strive to conceal him,
To blank him out,
But once he has made up his mind,
He is intent on having his way.

Incarcerated deep inside me,
He is like a hot flame,
Burning the pit of my stomach.
Sometimes he chokes me,
Leaves me gasping for breath
And that's when I give in.

I weaken
And he comes roaring out.

Francesca Lamberti (10)
Warren Road Primary School, Orpington

Anger

Anger is a wrath of fury,
Anger engulfs you and banishes other thoughts,
Anger is a raging bull, bulldozing everything in its path,
Anger is a dismal cloud, smothering all happiness,
Anger is like a volcano, erupting on its surroundings,
Anger takes over all consciousness.

Anger entwines itself on your body, completely controlling you,
Anger is like a gun; it shoots down your victim but never replenishes
your thirst,
Anger destroys all hope and joy,
Anger can slay weak hearts as if slicing butter,
Anger is a roaring fire and rarely gets put out,
Anger is a leopard; it skulks around and can strike at any time.

Anger can crush innocent souls without meaning to do so,
Anger can leave abruptly, but always lurks beneath your soul.

Matthew Massey (11)
Warren Road Primary School, Orpington

What?

Shadow trembler,
Darkness avoider,
Duvet hider.

Alert observer,
Crouching shiverer,
Evil eliminator.

Blood taster,
Lip biter,
Nail nibbler.

Teeth chatterer,
Wide-eyed watcher,
Deep breath taker.

Adrenaline rusher . . .

Amelia Morris (10)
Warren Road Primary School, Orpington

Est.1991

Young Writers Information

We hope you have enjoyed reading this book – and that you will continue to in the coming years.

If you're a young writer who enjoys reading and creative writing, or the parent of an enthusiastic poet or story writer, do visit our website www.youngwriters.co.uk. Here you will find free competitions, workshops and games, as well as recommended reads, a poetry glossary and our blog.

If you would like to order further copies of this book, or any of our other titles, then please give us a call or visit **www.youngwriters.co.uk.**

Young Writers
Remus House
Coltsfoot Drive
Peterborough
PE2 9BF
(01733) 890066 / 898110
info@youngwriters.co.uk